D1362759

Tales of the Snow Leopard

With contributions from

Khenrab Phuntsog, Smanla Tsering, the people of Hemis National Park, Philomène Verlaan

With illustrations by

Kitty Warnock, Philomène Verlaan

Compiled and produced by Philomène Verlaan

FIRST EDITION

ISBN-10: 1533612250
ISBN-13: 978-1533612250

Monastery Library NS/Kov 2015

TABLE OF CONTENTS

1

In Memoriam

Peter Matthiessen, whose enthralling book '*The Snow Leopard*'[1] first inspired us.

In Appreciation

Dr. George B. Schaller, whose unremitting dedication to the cause of conservation generally, and in the high Himalaya in particular, encourages us to persevere, because we agree that "the snow leopard might well serve as a symbol of man's commitment to the future of the mountain world,"[2] and we hope that its survival in harmony with the people of and visitors to Hemis National Park will contribute to achieving a sustainable future for our whole world.

"For everything that lives is holy, life delights in life."
William Blake (1793) in: '*America: A Prophecy*'

---

[1] Viking Press, New York, 1978.
[2] From 'The Snow Leopard,' in: '*Stones of Silence: Journeys in the Himalaya*' (Viking Press, New York, 1979) pp. 8-50 at p. 50.

FOREWORD

To an outsider like me, the snow leopard in the lonely grandeur of its mountain realm is a phantom which tantalizes with its presence, watching with frosty eyes from among the rock shadows, yet seldom revealing itself. It is rare and of exquisite beauty, and one wants to help protect it, but that is a difficult task. Throughout the twelve Asian countries where snow leopards occur they are shot, trapped and poisoned in retaliation for killing livestock. Deprived of their natural prey of wild sheep and goats, they may even enter poorly constructed and poorly guarded pens to kill the confined domestic animals. Government regulations to protect the endangered snow leopard are not enough. After all, livestock killed by snow leopards and other predators represent a considerable financial loss and threat to the livelihood of a household. Successful conservation strategies must provide social and economic benefits to local communities and this requires their whole-hearted participation.

Tales of the Snow Leopard relates the extraordinary success of such a conservation project in and around the Hemis National Park in Ladakh, India. Ladakhis recount how families in the Park changed their attitudes toward wildlife protection. It is now realized that wildlife and livestock can coexist if properly managed. The communities have also received various benefits from the Government of India, and from Indian and foreign organizations: electricity in homes, compensation for livestock killed by predators, restoration of temples, and promotion of tourism through well-

4

regulated homestays, to name a few. Instead of killing troublesome snow leopards, they can now call on rescue teams and veterinarians to solve problems. Of basic importance is that communities are intimately involved: it is **their** program.

The visions, ideas, and desires of local people are all too seldom recorded by projects. This book offers a happy exception in that it encouraged Ladakhis, especially elderly ones, to tell their stories. Communities now have information about their past and present, and future generations will have a history that would otherwise be lost in the rapidly changing cultures. We learn that a massive willow tree was not cut down for years because a Naga, a powerful snake spirit, lived in it. We also learn of the shepherdess Abi Choskiputit who built many stone mani walls, and of two monks who built a line of stupas. Such history not only adds immeasurably to a region's identity and ancient integrity, but also teaches everyone to value cultural traditions.

Local lamas are the spiritual advisers in the Hemis region, stressing compassion toward all living beings. Ladakhi folk songs also show much awareness of the environment, seeking blessings from the sun and moon to protect nature. On being interviewed, Sonam Dorjay noted that snow leopards "have a special magnetism and power." Indeed, everyone seems to rejoice in telling tales about meeting this benign cat. Yet there are gaps in perception. There are no folk songs about snow leopards. The wolf, a predator with a special beauty all its own, is feared or almost ignored in the tales. Nature is a circle, we must acknowledge, that includes everything from people to sheep to wolves, and it must not be broken.

Tales of the Snow Leopard is a superb contribution to the literature of nature and culture. I hope that the approach of this project will be emulated in many places to offer communities and all inhabitants, domestic and wild, a healthy and harmonious future.

I, too, have a tale of meeting a snow leopard, one from the Hindu Kush Mountains of Pakistan in 1970. The December cold gripped the valley in late afternoon. Far up a slope a female snow leopard reclined on a spur, her chin resting on a forepaw. She was guarding a kill, a domestic goat, and I had come to spend a night with her. When I slowly angled up the slope, she flattened into the rocks to monitor my approach. She then vanished in ghostly retreat, sinuously molding herself into the terrain. But bold and curious, she returned to her original spot when I unrolled my sleeping bag in full view of her about 150 feet away. I observed her feeding until darkness engulfed us. It snowed that night, heavy wet flakes that soaked through my sleeping bag. With first light, I saw her sitting dry and protected beneath a rock overhang.

Dr. George B. Schaller,
Panthera and Wildlife Conservation Society

KW 2015

REFLECTIONS

I have been visiting the area of the Hemis National Park since 1980. Although I have sometimes been an irregular visitor, I now know most of the families in Markha and Chilling-Sumda pretty well and have seen the YAFCAD[3] members grow up and start to contribute so effectively to their communities.

It was a tough world 35 years ago, but in many ways a wonderful one. Schools hardly worked even when they existed. Medical services were rudimentary. There were almost no roads. Life was hard for the families of these villages. If you fell ill, you went to Leh on a donkey or walked (impossible in winter), relied on the local Amchi, or died. Families depended on subsistence agriculture to survive, farming much more land than most of them do today. Most people stayed together in the village, if only because there was little alternative. Lest this sounds overly negative, community life was very strong. Families helped each other (and still do) at times of crisis and at festivals, and they came together for rituals in the village gompa. Although food was not as nutritious or varied as it might have been, nobody was seriously hungry. Above all it was a happy society. I recall so many evenings sitting round the fire in a smoky kitchen, with the snow coming in through the roof, but laughing and gossiping, discussing ideas, drinking certainly and often singing and dancing as well. However difficult the circumstances, the village people did their best to extract whatever fun they could from the situation.

---

[3] YAFCAD: the Youth Association For Conservation And Development – see Introduction.

It is worth remembering that in those days wildlife was often regarded as a nuisance, even a threat. A great deal of effort had to go into protecting livestock from predators, as these stories show. Keeping blue sheep[4] and other animals out of the fields was also important and sometimes hard work. The loss of a valuable animal or a field of ripening barley could mean a hungry winter. It is not surprising that some poaching of wild sheep and goats did take place and a snow leopard[5] that got in among the domestic flocks might be killed. But although confrontations did sometimes happen, I don't think anybody would have welcomed a valley where there were no blue sheep or ibex[6] or where the snow leopards never came. Although the Hemis National Park did not even exist in 1980, travelling through these valleys gave wonderful opportunities to see wildlife large and small and even to come across a snow leopard if you were lucky.

There have been many changes since those days; some are for the better, others are rather sad. Communications have improved, as have schools and health services. The old physical isolation has largely broken down and, partly as a result of this, people in these villages are now open to outside ideas, to education and to the world in general. Some visitors, I know, worry about this, fearing that too much change will destroy what is so wonderful in traditional Ladakh. I welcome many of these changes. It is hard to condemn roads when one has seen a woman being carried down an icy trail with a baby half in and half out of her body. It is hard to be against education when it is probably the only way in which young people can escape from a life as a labourer on the roads. What is much more of a worry to me is the growing difficulty in wresting a living from the land. Farming in the valleys of the Hemis National Park has

---

[4] Blue sheep: also known as bharal (*Pseudois nayaur*). The fascinating evolutionary and taxonomic position of this ungulate which, despite its common name in English, is now classified as being more goat than sheep, and the field work leading to this result, are described for the non-specialist reader by Dr. George Schaller, the pre-eminent expert on the wild sheep and goats of the Himalaya in, e.g., '*Mountain Monarchs*' (University of Chicago Press, Chicago, 1977) and '*Stones of Silence*' (*op. cit.*, n. 1).
[5] Snow leopard: *Panthera uncia* or *Uncia uncia*; *shan* in the Ladakhi language.
[6] Ibex: *Capra sibirica hemalayanus.*

always been hard; however, now not only is it even harder, but there are alternatives. Too many of these alternatives take people away from the village, threatening the long-term survival of this way of life.

One new alternative, which can contribute to the community, is wildlife tourism. Thanks to the enlightened work of the Government of India Wildlife Department and the enthusiasm of YAFCAD and the people of the Park, wildlife is better protected now and easier for visitors to see. The Hemis National Park will never, I hope, be like some places, where one can drive out in a Jeep, get your photograph and be home for tea. You still have to work for your sighting and long may that last.

But I question whether these villages can survive on tourism alone, beneficial though it is, and I believe that three things have to happen if a way of life that is important to the world is to continue into the future. The first is to improve facilities: health care, education, clean water, electricity. This is already happening. Second, agriculture needs to be revived. This will probably mean finding new crops or products which are sellable in local or wider markets. Much work is being done, especially by non-governmental organizations (NGOs), but it is not going to be easy in a globalizing world. Finally, all of us need to work together to preserve the village communities. This means finding jobs for the village people, either in the village or connected to the village. It means preserving and building the village culture, both religious and social. Fundamentally, it means making village life attractive and worthwhile for people who have growing experience of alternative ways of life. Is this possible?

Time will tell, but all of us must try. This book will help by preserving and popularizing stories that are part of the culture of a changing Ladakh. Although much will depend on government policy and actions, YAFCAD and other NGOs can do much by listening to the people of the Park and helping them to meet their aspirations in sustainable ways. They deserve our support. What can we others do? We can help to make Ladakh better known (back to this book!). We can perhaps offer practical support, as many already do, but we must try not to interfere. It will be the ideas and work of the people of the Park which will preserve their way of life in a changing world and our job is to help where we can.

How might we judge success? I hope we can see an area where villages are thriving again, where wildlife is part of an integrated world where it is welcomed as a contributor to the way of life and not, ever, seen as a threat, as was too often the case in the past. YAFCAD and their friends have an important role to play if this is to happen. I wish them luck.[7]

Sir Robert ffolkes Bt OBE

---

[7] Sir Robert ffolkes Bt OBE set up and ran the Save the Children Fund's program in Ladakh for many years; now retired, he returns yearly to Ladakh, where he is highly esteemed throughout the region. He is a mentor to Khenrab and Smanla. His moving and insightful documentary, "Taming The Dragon: Development and Change in Sumdha, Ladakh," produced with Namgyal Thankthong, and soon to be released, is warmly recommended.

How The Snow Leopard Got Its Tales

Khenrab Phuntsog and Smanla Tsering, Ladakhi wildlife rangers employed by the Wildlife Service of the Government of India, have primary responsibility for the approximately 50-60 snow leopards roaming in Hemis National Park. Here they were born and raised, Khenrab in the village of Chilling and Smanla in the village of Markha, and here they live with their families on their ancestral lands. Steeped in snow leopard science and snow leopard lore gained over many years of personal and professional experience, as well as being known or related to every one of the 162 families in Hemis National Park, Khenrab and Smanla embody a living treasure trove of active knowledge about the Park, its people, its culture, and its natural history. Their non-profit foundation, the Youth Association For Conservation And Development (YAFCAD), is dedicated to the socially, culturally and environmentally responsible evolution of Hemis National Park. Staffed entirely by volunteers, most of whom are young people from the Park, YAFCAD undertakes projects that include: temple restoration, installation of renewable energy systems and electrification,[8] homestay[9] development, waste management, ecotourism, agriculture and animal husbandry, and setting up centers run by local women providing clean filtered drinking water, locally made food and their own handicrafts to visitors.

---

[8] The 21 villages in Hemis National Park now (June 2016) have solar-powered electricity. YAFCAD was immeasurably assisted in this achievement by the generous expert assistance of Jean-François Chanteux, Niyamdru Dro and Electriciens Sans Frontières.

[9] The homestay concept was pioneered in the village of Rumbak (nine families) by the Snow Leopard Conservancy India Trust and further developed by YAFCAD in Hemis National Park, with support by the Government of India Wildlife Department. Today all the villages in the Park offer homestay facilities.

Philo, an oceanographer/lawyer with the University of Hawai'i at Mānoa, met Khenrab while celebrating a Very Big Birthday by wandering around Ladakh, accompanied by five women friends she had enticed along. Now this world holds many Ladies Who Lunch, but only a few Ladies Who Ladakh, and Philo considered herself to be especially fortunate that her friends included some of this latter select set. The interests of the Ladies Who Ladakh being highly diverse, she asked Steve Berry (MD of the UK company, Mountain Kingdoms, which organized the logistics for the Ladies with the help in Leh of T. Wangchuk Kalon, MD of the Ladakhi company, Snow Leopard Trails) to recommend a local guide deeply versed in all matters Ladakhi. Thus the Ladies met Khenrab, on leave from his day job to do some YAFCAD work in the Park, and whose route coincided with theirs.

Khenrab and the Ladies embarked on a tapestry of conversations on topics ranging as widely as Ladakh's magnificent mountains are high and continuing unabated until their last evening back in Leh. Especially intriguing were Khenrab's occasional vignettes about seemingly unexceptional features of the Ladakhi landscape – a tree, a series of walls, a confluence of rivers, a dilapidated hut, a misty pass – they offered tantalizing glimpses of a subtle embroidery that transmuted the tapestry into an intricately brocaded carpet of stories flying about Hemis National Park. Before long, Khenrab and the Ladies decided an ideal YAFCAD project would be to collect, publish and sell these stories for the benefit of future generations of Ladakhis and to enhance the experience of visitors to the Park.

However, these stories had never been told to non-Ladakhis before, or written down for publication. Khenrab first had to obtain permission to do this from the people of the Park. They consented enthusiastically, and urged him to hurry, for those who still knew the stories in their entirety were mostly very old and would soon be gone. Philo agreed to help write the English version of the stories.

In return (Philo is no altruist), she requested that Khenrab show her a snow leopard, because none had deigned to appear, to the

Ladies' deep disappointment, during her Very Big Birthday trip. Khenrab considered this a fair deal and the Tales of the Snow Leopard began to grow.

Recounting snippets of the Tales to the Ladies Who Ladakh was quite easy, but seriously pursuing those Tales to ensure they were correct, complete and properly sourced, ethnographically speaking, was a far more difficult task, adding a further layer of complexity to Khenrab's already very full life. He enlisted Smanla to help collect Tales while they worked in the Park.

Conveying the Tales to Philo was the next challenge. Khenrab and Smanla invited her to join the field segment of a YAFCAD project to instruct young YAFCAD members living in the Park in its natural history and in snow leopard spotting. These skills would significantly increase their employability as visitor guides, and their income. Finding employment in the Park is difficult for young people, and providing them with sustainable options is a major YAFCAD objective.

The project included a mid-winter week under canvas at Husing, a remote snow leopard crossroads in the Park, near the main path to Rumbak village, where Khenrab and Smanla, who developed and conducted the project, also deploy camera "traps" and engage in other snow leopard observational activities for the Wildlife Department. Field work went on by day, greatly assisted by a spotting scope and binoculars kindly donated by Swarovski Optik, and in the evenings after dinner everyone gathered in the mess tent to exchange Tales.

Comments and questions by the apprentice YAFCAD rangers, by miscellaneous Ladakhi travellers passing through Husing, and by Philo, generated more Tales and suggestions for further sources of Tales. When the Husing field work was done, Khenrab, Smanla and Philo set out to ground-truth the new Tales and visit potential storytellers, who were scattered around the Park in remote villages far from any roadhead.

Particularly striking to Philo was the prevalence of snow leopards in these Tales. No matter what subject the teller originally set out to address, sooner or later a snow leopard usually appeared, even if only briefly, attesting to the complexity of the relationship between the people of Hemis National Park and their famous fellow feline residents. The Ladakhis say that the snow leopard has the strength of nine strong men, the beauty of nine beautiful women, and the wisdom of nine wise men. In the Park one is constantly aware of the presence of snow leopards, regardless of whether they are actually visible to our limited faculties, especially as they are exquisitely designed to be wholly camouflaged. Even when they are up close and technically in plain sight, they are very easily missed. Snow leopard spotting is an arcane high art.

Philo thought her Hawaiian friends might well consider the snow leopard to be a type of *'aumakua*, a guardian being of the Park as a whole, rather than of any one individual or family. So these are Tales of – and for – the snow leopard, who often slinks through them itself, but always watches, with its iceberg-blue eyes, while they are told.

TALES OF THE SNOW LEOPARD

Khenrab's First Snow Leopards

"My very first snow leopard appeared when I was seven years old, while I played on the roof of our house in Chilling village. It crouched on a cliff staring down at me, and it didn't move even when I yelled 'Big cat, big cat!' I didn't know it was a snow leopard yet. My father, Tsewang Gurmet, Gongma House, came out to have a look, and told me it was a snow leopard, and we chased it away, because it might attack our livestock.

"The second snow leopard I saw when I was about twelve. My grandmother, Phuntsok Dolma, had just died and I was helping Tashi Tundup, a painter from Bagothang House, and Tsering Phuntsok from Yokma House, prepare her cremation mound in the cemetery grounds in the valley next to Chilling village. The cremation mound is a re-usable brick structure with a metal plate on top for the body. When the cremation is complete, the ashes are taken to the mountains to blow away with the wind. Each family has its own mound, which is decorated with Buddhist symbols. If no deaths have occurred for some time, the mound usually needs some rebuilding and repainting.

"After we had been working for a couple of hours, Phuntsok noticed some blue sheep on a slope above us and pointed out a snow leopard sneaking up to them. It launched into three long, sinewy leaps towards the last of the sheep, but narrowly missed its catch. All the blue sheep sprang away over the ridge. We kept watching, because now we were concerned about our own livestock grazing on that slope. The snow leopard crouched down for a while, gazing straight at us. Then it loped languidly up to the top of the ridge, its long tail streaming straight out behind it, and disappeared over the edge where the sheep had gone. Satisfied that it was hunting the blue sheep, Tashi resumed his painting and Phuntsok and I continued rebuilding the grave.

"Suddenly we saw the snow leopard again. It had reappeared over the ridge right above our livestock, evidently intent on finding its dinner there instead of among the blue sheep. We all started yelling and waving, but although the snow leopard heard and saw us perfectly well, it clearly didn't care at all, because we were too far away. Phuntsok and I started running up the ridge towards our herd, still shouting and gesticulating at the snow leopard. Tashi kept on painting, but carried on screaming at it too.

"Then I saw that the snow leopard had already killed and was eating a fat black goat. The rest of our herd stood stock still, watching. Phuntsok and I approached, but the snow leopard ignored us until Phuntsok got close enough to throw a big stone which hit its flank. Only then did it quit eating and leave, most reluctantly. Phuntsok identified the goat as belonging to my family, so I chivvied the rest of the herd down to their pen and Phuntsok carried the carcass. During all this activity, Tashi continued painting and yelling. This was the first time I realized how clever snow leopards can be: they can develop a strategy, plan an ambush, and hide behind a ridge, so people in the Park, as Tashi, Phuntsok and I realized when the snow leopard played out the strategy with us, can't see them going after our livestock."

Ancestor Tree

Not all trees in Ladakh are created equal. Some must be treated with particular care and reverence, regardless of any personal inconvenience this might cause. The Ladies received a first inkling of this significant arboreal constraint on Ladakhi life in Chilling village. Khenrab chatted with a man under a beautiful willow tree, while the Ladies admired the tree in their several ways – sketching, photographing and gazing. The two men, however, warily circled the tree, shaking their heads, clicking their teeth, and frowning at it as they talked. On rejoining the Ladies, Khenrab remarked that the tree was causing major problems for his friend's house, but he couldn't cut it down, because it was sacred to his ancestors. When Khenrab returned later to request permission to add the story of the tree to the Tales, his friend began by introducing himself and his life.

"I am Tsewang Rigzen, son of Rinchen Paldan, of Chikpa House, Chilling. When I was young, Chilling was very difficult to reach. The trails were narrow. The nearest place to cross the Zanskar River was near Alchi, so a big detour via there and Nimmo village was necessary to reach Leh. Just getting to Leh could take a week. I first went to Leh when I was about six years old for the Hemis Festival, riding on my father's shoulders because I was too small to walk fast. We had no homestays then; on the way to Leh we spent the nights in caves and in the houses of friends and family. In Leh we stayed in a courtyard. Leh was small with a few interesting shops, but I remember especially my first sight of cars there. I was fascinated with how the cars grew bigger as they came closer and became smaller as they went away. This I will never forget. My first ride was in a jeep from Leh to Hemis Monastery, where I saw my first masked dance.

"When I was about eight years old my family chose me to study in a school the government had just opened in Chilling. Unfortunately the school closed after two years and I didn't learn much, because the teacher thought I was too young. During this time I was only allowed to draw Chilling Palace and learn the Ladakhi alphabet. My father is a coppersmith, so when the school closed I helped him by operating the bellows to fan the fire. I also learned how to shape metal objects with small hammers. When the school reopened after a few years I returned to it and now I was allowed to learn more. I could not go away for further study because I am the eldest son. I stayed in Chilling to manage the family land and livestock, and I became a coppersmith like my father.

"Part of managing livestock is keeping the flock safe from wolves and snow leopards. Wolves come often to Chilling. I spotted my first wolf there. While I was telling my aunt, Tsetan Palkit, who was teaching me how to be a shepherd, about it, we heard people shouting that a wolf was killing a sheep. My aunt and I sprinted to where we kept the sheep. I ran so fast I tripped and fell and I hurt my nose. I ignored the blood pouring from my nose and reached the place before my aunt, and found the wolf still on the sheep's carcass. As my aunt arrived I snatched the carcass from the wolf, which ran away. We gave the carcass to the family who owned the sheep so they could eat it. The wolf scared me so much that it took me a long time to be confident enough to go up by myself to the high pastures as a shepherd. I made a good slingshot to help control the herd and keep away the wolves and I learned to be a crack shot. Now as a shepherd I take turns with other families to lead all the livestock up to the high pastures to graze.

"The first time I saw a snow leopard was in the high pastures when I was very young, with my aunt, learning how to be a shepherd. I only remember that the snow leopard had a huge head. We have a saying in Ladakh that we should not talk about snow leopards while we are shepherding, because we think that will attract them. But it is okay to talk about ghosts, because we believe ghosts will then keep away.

"We have many special folk songs in Chilling. My mother, Tundup Tsomo, was always singing them and she taught them all to me. I sing them to myself during the day when I am alone up in the mountains with the herd. I think these days of singing in the

18

mountains are the best days of my life. I have become a good singer and very knowledgeable about our traditional folk songs. I have a large repertoire of them now. But we have no songs about snow leopards, or about any other predators on our livestock, such as wolves.

"As my parents got older I assumed more responsibilities. My marriage was arranged with a nice girl from Kaya, Phuntsok Dolma. I looked for other sources of income and decided to make my house larger for my family and to have rooms for homestay guests.

"Close by my house is a huge willow tree, which was planted long ago when the house was built. I hadn't noticed this tree much until a big branch collapsed into my neighbor Tsering Dawa's field (Gatseringpa House) and interfered with his ploughing. The branch was still attached to the tree. My parents said we couldn't cut it off, because a Naga lives in the tree and cutting the branch would bring bad luck to the whole village, and especially to my neighbor and to us. We left the branch obstructing the field until it naturally detached itself from the tree, and then my neighbor moved it.

"Meanwhile, I examined this Naga tree more closely. Another huge branch held a large crow's nest and hung perilously close to my brand-new guest room. Every time the wind blew, this branch creaked loudly, the crows screeched angrily and I was terrified the branch would break off and fall into the guest room and onto the guests. I began building a new guest room, on the other side of the house, but meanwhile I had to put guests in the dangerous and noisy guest room. Every night I had a guest in there I stayed awake all night praying for no wind.

"Even with the new guest room finished, this tree caused other problems. It blocked the sun from my house, other branches threatened my neighbor's field, its trunk blocked the footpath to my house, and its roots were undermining the house foundations. It was clear that this tree was originally planted much too near the house, and so maybe it could be cut down. There would be ways to propitiate the Naga.

"But when I asked my parents who planted this tree, they said it was probably some of our ancestors, although they couldn't remember precisely who. My parents didn't think the tree could be cut down, because the ancestors might not have been reborn yet. So the tree not only has a Naga living in it who would rage at the village and cause misfortune if it were felled, but even more crucially it was planted by ancestors who needed the tree in order to be reborn. But as we didn't know exactly who planted it, we couldn't find out if they have been reborn either.

"We consulted the most eminent lamas visiting Chilling to conduct services in the temple. Chilling does not have its own resident lama. The first lama (the Twelfth Incarnation of His Holiness Gyalwang Drukpa) we consulted agreed to examine the tree. After doing so he blessed it and assured us that he took the full responsibility upon himself that nothing bad would happen to the village if the tree were cut down. But I got nervous and in the end I didn't dare to do it.

"But the tree kept causing us more and more problems, so when another eminent lama came to Chilling we also asked him what to do. He performed the same rituals and made the same promises as the Twelfth Incarnation, so I now felt confident to go ahead with felling it, but this time my family wouldn't allow it.

"The Twelfth Incarnation visited Chilling again in 2012 and stayed in Chilling's gompa overnight. We asked him to examine and bless the tree once more so we could cut it down at last. After spending some time with the tree, he decided that after all it would be very difficult to cut it down.

"So I gave up on cutting down the tree. Instead I began to move the house away from it. This is difficult and expensive and is taking a long time. What is particularly frustrating for me is that every New Year's Day I must prepare and offer elaborate and expensive food offerings to the ancestors in order to honor them and pay my respects. Even with all the problems with that tree I have done this faithfully every year and always with the best food. But I can't help wondering why I am doing this, considering all the trouble the tree they planted is causing me. Also I constantly ask myself whether I am not wasting my time completely, because my ancestors might be reborn by now, so the tree would no longer be necessary."

Two years later, in December 2015, Khenrab and Philo were back in Chilling working on the Tales. They observed the Ancestor Tree still flourishing mightily by Tsewang Rigzen's house, and asked him for an update.

Tsewang Rigzen: "Oh yes, this tree is still causing me big problems. For example, a snow leopard got into my pen and killed 25 sheep and goats. At first I thought this was a blessing, because I had been wanting to get rid of this flock as they are so much trouble to manage now, but I couldn't have them butchered because that would bring bad karma to me, and also my parents didn't want me to sell them. But because they were killed by a snow leopard, it was not my fault, so no bad karma for me. Also I would get compensation from the State Wildlife Department.[10] I cut up the carcasses for the

---

[10]An essential contribution to snow leopard conservation in the Park is the Government of India's enlightened policy of compensating livestock owners for the loss of any of their flock killed by snow leopards. In return, the villagers do not kill snow leopards, even if they are caught in the pen. Instead, they call the Government of India's snow leopard rescue service, currently implemented by Khenrab and Smanla, assisted by their colleagues in the State Wildlife Department, to remove the snow leopard from the pen. Taken to Leh for

meat, but there was so much meat I couldn't use it all and I gave meat to all the families in Chilling. They were very grateful and in return gave me live sheep and goats in return. So now I have an even bigger herd and even more problems.

"Still, I remained patient with the tree for some more time, but finally I appealed to the Twelfth Incarnation for new ideas about the tree once more. He recommended consulting His Eminence Tokden Rinpoche, who is more qualified to deal with Nagas, and I invited him to Chilling to examine the tree. His Eminence came earlier this year, performed prayers at the tree, and assured me that now I could safely cut it down and nothing bad would happen. So I am planning to do this soon."

The next morning Tsewang Rigzen visited Khenrab's elder brother, Tsewang Gonbo, who is a coppersmith, to borrow an enormous axe, which he sharpened and fixed firmly into its wooden handle. That afternoon, Khenrab and Philo watched Tsewang Rigzen begin chopping down the Ancestor Tree.

examination by a vet and treated if injured, when it is healed, it is released back into the wild. See also the Tale 'Caring For Rescued Snow Leopards' in this book.

War In Chilling

Even though it is only 400 years old, Chilling village, with its six families, is agreeably integrated into its spectacular surroundings, as are all the villages in the Park. The only odd buildings in Chilling are two large oblong concrete structures, one on each side of the Zanskar River.

Philo: "These look like bunkers. Why are bunkers in this peaceful Chilling?"

Khenrab: "The war came to Chilling once. One of our elders still remembers it all. I will find out what happened from him."

This kindly gentleman, Rinchen Paldan, set the scene as elaborately as did his son, Tsewang Rigzen, Khenrab's friend of the Ancestor Tree.

"I am Rinchen Paldan of Chikpa House, Chilling. My childhood was difficult. I had few clothes, little food and no education. At the age of eight I began to help as a shepherd. As I was the eldest son, when I was 12 my family sent me to the workshop of Meme Phuntsok, a coppersmith in Chilling, to learn the craft of copper work. To honor the craftsman who was to be my teacher, even though it was not far, I went to his house mounted correctly on a horse, bringing khatas, incense and a chabskan as gifts. For the first time in my life I felt like a king.

"Soon after I joined him, my teacher took me to Leh to live in the household of a wealthy family while we made a set of special copper teapots for them. This was the first time I had left Chilling. We went to Leh on foot, via Alchi, because it was not possible to cross the Zanskar River near Chilling. It was a long journey. As an apprentice, I was not paid, but the family gave me clothes and shoes and different types of food – especially rice and sweet tea, which were not available in Chilling then. I really liked the food in Leh.

"During my apprenticeship I became good at crafting plain surfaces and beautiful finishes in copper, but no matter how hard I tried, I just couldn't do any intricate designs. My teacher was very frustrated with me and pushed me hard. He kept saying that I just wasn't concentrating. I was frustrated too. I experimented with drawing designs on wood and stone using charcoal, and at night I dreamed about creating perfect designs, and I even talked in my sleep about designs, but when I woke up my designs were just as clumsy as before. I concluded that not being able to do designs was just my bad luck and I decided to become an expert at making the most exquisite plain surfaces.

"Meanwhile my parents retired and I became the head of our house, which brought me new responsibilities. Most difficult was paying the tax to the government: we regularly had to send wood, charcoal, wheat and barley on the back of a donkey or dzo from Chilling to the government store in Leh. I realized these items were being given to government employees for their heating and food. My father had done this until now; until it became my duty I didn't know this was a required expense I had to provide for.

"My teacher and I both travelled widely for our copper work. Besides Leh, we worked in monasteries and in other villages. We did this in winter and in the middle of summer – the times of year when no farming needed to be done. Otherwise I helped with the farm and the livestock. I especially liked going up to the high pastures with the flocks for grazing, with the clean air and so many flowers. All the shepherds from the families would make cheese and butter together, and I did some copper work up there too.

"The grazing times were always lovely and peaceful, especially early in the grazing season, when the animals that don't give milk, like dzos, go up first, usually a month before the others. They don't need so many shepherds then, so only two go up at a time. They stay in a two-room hut, sharing one room and keeping the other free for travellers who need a place to spend the night.

"One year I was up in the high pastures early with another shepherd. At the end of the day we couldn't find one of the bulls. We looked everywhere for it, but gave up when it got too dark. We hoped the bull would survive the night and we would find him in the morning, because otherwise the owner from the big Yokma House in Chilling would be very angry. We had begun making dinner in our hut when we heard strange noises coming from the room next door. We thought it was a snow leopard that had gotten in there somehow. The door of that room was closed and we didn't dare open it.

"The next morning we sent a message to Sumdachenmo, the nearest village, for help in dealing with the snow leopard. It would be furious and frightened and hungry and thirsty, as by now it was the afternoon of the second day of its captivity. We would probably have to kill it, because we would have little chance of not getting hurt ourselves as the big cat sprang out when we opened the door. This was long before we had the snow leopard rescue service we have now.

"Eventually three men from Sumda arrived, one old, one young and one rich. The old one and the young one chattered happily about how they would spend the reward money they would receive for killing the snow leopard.[11] The old one planned to buy enough food for a whole year and the young one intended to get a warm track suit in Leh. The rich one said nothing, but handed the young one an ancient firearm which still required powder being pushed down its barrel.

"The young one poked the loaded rifle through a small hole in the door and peered along the barrel. The hole was just big enough for him to report seeing a large, moist, black, and utterly unfeline nose sniffing the muzzle. We suddenly realized that our missing bull might have got into that room. A peek through the hole met an enraged bull's eye. The three Sumda men went weak at the knees with relief that they hadn't shot the bull, especially the young one, who would have pulled the trigger. Instead of spending lots of reward money they would have been doling out compensation money to the bull's owners, and the young one would have bad karma from killing it. We two shepherds felt very foolish, but I was happy there was no snow leopard so we wouldn't have to kill it.

"One spring day we heard that soldiers from Pakistan were going to arrive in Chilling. We decided to send the women and

---

[11] This event also occurred long before the snow leopard was granted protected status and the compensation scheme was initiated by the Government of India.

children away to Khar, an isolated high valley above Chilling pu,[12] for safety. Every day we sent food up to them from the village. But after a week nothing had happened. A friend and I walked to the high pasture of Lanak to ask the shepherds up there whether they had seen anything. Because we didn't have any guns, we borrowed a big sword from the family of Khenrab Phuntsog, of Gongma House, to take with us. That family still keeps that sword today.[13] It was getting dark when we reached the top of the Taknak Pass, where we spent the night, without even a sleeping bag. At dawn we saw the shepherds letting the herds out of their night enclosure, so it seemed safe to go down there. The shepherds had seen nothing so far, but then an old man from Sumdachenmo village came up and said the soldiers from Pakistan were on their way and everyone was in a panic. He said the Sumdachenmo villagers had taken their valuables to the remote Umlung Valley and that they were right behind him, fleeing to the Alam Valley, opposite the Tilaat Valley,[14] on the other side of the Zanskar River.

"Our women and children had returned to Chilling by the time we got back, but the very next day soldiers from Pakistan arrived and occupied Gongma House. Helped by people from Markha, Kaya and Skiu villages, the Indian army set up camp on the other side of the Zanskar River. They couldn't cross it because there was no bridge and the summer flow was high and swift. All Chilling's women and children now sheltered in Yokma House. Then the two sides began shooting at each other. After a week the Pakistani army moved higher up to Sanak, a stretch of irrigated land belonging to Yokma House, about two hours walk away. The Pakistani army forced the villagers to provide goats for milk, and goats and sheep for meat. Everyone, including me, was forced to help the Pakistani army. They looked like people from Skardu and Gilgit. They were very strong and quite kind; they gave food to the village people and we thought perhaps they were also being forced to fight which maybe they didn't want to do either, any more than

---

[12] Chilling pu: upper Chilling.
[13] This double-edged sword has a simple steel hilt, is 4.5 feet long and extremely heavy.
[14] The Tilaat Valley runs parallel to the Markha Valley, all the way to Nimaling.

we wanted to help them or fight them. Both sides built stone-walled bunkers with holes for guns.

"During the impasse caused by the swollen river, the villagers tried to continue their life. To grind flour at the village mill, they had to pass quite far along the Zanskar River from Chilling to the flying fox box bridge (trolley), on whose other side the path to the Markha Valley begins. The Indian army asked their local helpers where the Chilling villagers were going with those bags, and they replied – incorrectly – that they were providing flour to the Pakistani army. The Indian army began warning the Chilling villagers not to go to the mill. Meme Norbu from Yokma House ignored the warning, and also the warning shots from the Indian army, and only stopped when an Indian army bullet went straight through one cheek of his face and out the other. I watched his wound being cleaned – it was very painful. They passed a thick rough thread made of goat fiber back and forth through the wound in both cheeks like dental floss. Rinchen Sonam of Gongma House, Khenrab Phuntsog's grandfather, produced a small vial of highly precious musk from the musk deer.[15] They rubbed it on the wound and he drank some of it dissolved in water. He recovered completely, but on one side the wound never fully closed, so when he spoke and drank he had to block the hole with a paste made of tsampa and salted butter tea.

"We in Chilling figured out how to help the Indian army while they were stuck on the other side of the Zanskar River waiting for it to go down. The army needed to know how many Pakistani soldiers were in the village, in Sanak and in the bunkers, where they were and how and when they moved between these sites. We provided these details in Tibetan script on cloth wrapped around stones and lobbed across the river with a slingshot. My slingshot experience from shepherding came in very useful here.

"In the autumn, when the Zanskar River went down at last, the Indian army made boats from inflated cow, yak and dzo skins and crossed at the confluence of the Zanskar and Markha Rivers.

---

[15] Musk deer: *Moschus leucogaster* or *Moschus chrysogaster*; it is highly endangered. Musk (derived from Sanskrit, *muska*, meaning testicle) is secreted from a gland found only in adult males and is probably used to attract mates. Prized for its alleged pharmaceutical, aphrodisiac and cosmetic properties, it is extremely valuable.

This is a holy site with a stupa, one of three stupas[16] built in the time of King Kanishka. The Indian army headed for the Alam Valley via Lamayuru, to attack from behind the Pakistani army that was holed up in Chilling. The Pakistani army left Chilling for Lamayuru at the same time. They walked straight into the Indian army there and surrendered. There was no more fighting at Chilling, but the bunkers remain on both sides of the river to remind us of the time when the war came to our village."

---

[16] The other two Kanishka stupas are in Sani (Zanskar) and in Teri (Phu). This site is known as Lama Guru; it marks the spot where Guru Rinpoche (Padmasambhava, the 8th-century Indian sage and mystic who is credited with revitalizing Buddhism in Ladakh and Tibet) finally killed a demon he was chasing throughout Ladakh. The people from Markha and Chilling come with a monk twice a year, in the spring and summer, for a day-long ceremony. Body parts of this demon and signs of the titanic struggle are found scattered around the Park: the heart is near Chilling, and near the main road back to Leh a line of its petrified red blood runs along a yellow mountain slope into a rock ridge sliced in two by Guru Rinpoche to reveal the demon hiding behind it. Opposite the cloven rock, a small shrine of flags covers a nook in another rock face where a stupa image has naturally formed on a smooth boulder.

Master of Metal

Khenrab: "The word 'Chilling' means 'outsider.' Long ago Nepali craftsmen were invited to come decorate temples and stupas in Ladakh. Once their work was done, they were allowed to stay in Ladakh if they wanted to. Nepali metalsmiths founded Chilling. They couldn't decide where to set up the village, so one of them shot an arrow in the air and built the first house of Chilling, Yokma House, where it landed. This arrow is still kept in Yokma House.

"My grandfather, Rinchen Sonam, is a metal craftsman. He travelled all over Ladakh and made metal decorations for at least 30 temple stupas. His metal work is very distinctive, and easily recognized in Ladakh. He is very old now but still works every day in his studio in our house in Chilling. This is his Tale."

"I am Rinchen Sonam, son of Padma Lhundup, of Gongma House, Chilling. I am a younger son. Because of this I was not given good jobs but much hard work – mostly farming and shepherding. I was sent to herd the flocks from a very young age with an older relative. We had to make and repair our own shoes, which were of goat and yak wool. Mine always wore out quickly from running all over the rocks and rough trails after our herds. I couldn't keep up with the repairs, and the stones made my feet bleed.

"My eldest brother, Skarma Namgyal, became the apprentice of Meme Phuntsog Spalzang, of Yokma House, a master metal craftsman in Chilling. The apprenticeship was blessed in a big ceremony. I was very envious, and asked my mother, Kungzom Yangskit, 'When will it be my turn to go?' and my mother replied, 'Never.' At that moment I made a solemn internal promise to myself that I would learn to work with metal and be better than my brother.

"My father brought me a pair of rubber shoes and for a while I stopped envying my brother. The shoes were so splendid I didn't use them for two weeks, but when I finally did put them on, I got so worried about spoiling them on the hard terrain in the mountains and during the farming that I put them away and only used them for special occasions in the village. Once when I came back from the mountains, limping on my bleeding feet, my mother gave me sweet tea to help me forget the pain. I had never drunk tea sweetened with sugar before (usually we drank salted butter tea) and I still remember to this day how delicious it tasted. So as not to waste any of the tea leaves, I was very careful to soak them until all their 'tea-ness' was gone and the water was clear. Then I chewed the tea leaves afterwards to keep the taste even longer.

"When my eldest brother opened his metal workshop I went to observe and to help him as often as I could. I especially tried to memorize the designs. We had no pencil and paper, so I copied the designs from my memory in dust and soot on the stones around the fire in our kitchen. My brother realized that I was going to observe and help him whether he liked it or not, so he gradually began to teach me some of the techniques.

"When the Pakistani soldiers invaded Chilling, they moved into Gongma House, using the lower part of the house as a mess and kitchen and ignoring the workshop. Only my eldest brother and the old people were left in Gongma House. I no longer had to take care of the herds up in the pastures because the Pakistani soldiers were taking them for food, so my family decided to just let the flocks roam in the village. We had to take food up to the Pakistani army in the bunkers overlooking the village until their mess shifted from our house to Sanak. For a while a lot of shooting went on and small bombs exploded everywhere – one even exploded close to the house.[17]

"By autumn life had returned to normal in Chilling, but I didn't have to go back to the mountains because the Pakistani army had taken all our animals. All that autumn and winter I learned more metal work, studying with my brother and with other metal craftsmen in the village who were now also beginning to teach me a little bit. I learned very fast, twice as fast as anyone else, but

---

[17] See also the Tale 'War In Chilling' in this book.

everyone kept saying 'You are only a younger son, you must return to the fields.' This I refused to do. Instead, I challenged my brother to a metal pot design competition, in which our parents were the judges. Our parents decided mine was better, especially the design. Then my father relented at last and asked Tsetan Wangbo of Garsingpa House, a master tool craftsman, to make me a set of good tools. As I became more expert, I began to develop a reputation in other villages for metal work, especially in copper, silver and gold, and I set up my own workshop. I was also given more responsibility for the family.

"My own house was collapsing, so I learned carpentry and masonry to repair it myself. I even restored all the woodwork, including the designs. Now I had become a fully qualified craftsman. The Yokma House family then invited me to restore their old house and build their new one. I did this. But above all I am a metalsmith.

"I built my first stupa for our family temple in Gongma House. I constructed the inner wooden frame and its highly ornate exterior, decorated with gold, silver, turquoise and red coral. The turquoise and coral pieces were taken from my grandmother's perak.[18] Then I built a stupa for the Chilling village temple, for which I also used precious metals and other valuable materials. I began receiving invitations to build stupas in homes and monasteries in other places in Ladakh, including Lamayuru, Markha, Stakna, and Changtang. I travelled everywhere to complete these commissions – in all I built 32 gold and silver temple stupas in Ladakh. I also made countless metal ritual objects, including dorjes and bells, as well as metal kettles, bowls and pots.

"I brought home many gifts for the village and for my family from the places I visited during my working trips. For example, I brought the first pressure cooker to Chilling. I bought it in Leh, and the salesman there explained to me how to use it. He said it was very simple: 'After two whistles the food is ready.' So I invited the whole village to a demonstration and a trial meal straight from the pressure cooker in Yokma House, the only house in Chilling big enough to host everyone.

"The whole village came splendidly dressed up in their best traditional robes and hats and sat down in an expectant circle around

---

[18] See also the Tales 'Amchi And Bear' and 'Perak' in this book.

the stove, apprehensively watching this loudly hissing and vibrating pot. The two whistles made everyone jump twice, but I said: 'Don't worry, this means it is ready.' But I couldn't get the lid off. I tried and tried, and because the salesman hadn't told me about this possibility, I finally decided the lid was stuck, whacked the top hard with a big hammer, and forced the stopper through into the cooker. A huge blast of scalding steam rocketed out and food exploded around the room, covering the floors, walls, windows, ceiling and all the people of Chilling.

"Everyone laughed at me and I was very angry that the salesman had not given me good instructions about how to release the pressure first before opening the cooker. The women became afraid of this contraption. It was a long time before anyone else in Chilling bought a pressure cooker. Even when everyone learned how to use it correctly they stayed nervous while it was cooking and couldn't relax until it was safely opened. The grandmother of Chikpa House, Tundup Tsomo,[19] still runs outside as soon as she hears the first whistle and only comes back in the house when they call from the kitchen that everything is finished and the pot is safely open.

"During my next trip to Leh I bought a lamp for Chilling. Because of the experience with the pressure cooker, I made very sure the salesman told me exactly how it worked and showed me everything in detail, because I planned to give a party for the village to demonstrate the lamp, and I wanted everything to be perfect. Again everybody came and sat in a circle around the lamp, silent and fully concentrated on the various procedures I had to do to get it ready. I had practiced several times with the salesman and I was very confident. When everything was prepared I made the room dark and lit the lamp. The whole village gasped as the light began to glow. I was very proud that it was working. As it shone more brightly an old man reached over and touched the bulb, just slightly, but the light instantly went out. I realized that I hadn't bought a spare bulb. It was the one thing I had not planned for. We had to hold the light party in the dark. Again I was embarrassed, and the village teased me about 'bringing big light but only for a few seconds.'

---

[19] Tsewang Rigzen's mother; see also the Tale 'Ancestor Tree' in this book.

32

Kitchen NS/KW

"My luck with introducing useful inventions to the village finally improved when I brought home a radio. Sumdachenmo village[20] had received the very first radio in this part of Ladakh. As soon as my niece, Mentok Lhazes,[21] heard about this box that produced voices and music, she and all her friends – essentially the whole younger generation from Chilling – walked over two high passes[22] to see and listen to it. When they returned from Sumdachenmo she begged me to buy one. She is my favourite niece, whom I raised like a daughter, and as I cannot refuse her anything, I had a radio with me the next time I came back from Leh. Because this was Chilling's first radio (we called it a transistor then), everyone in the village came to Gongma House to listen to it. I dressed up in my full traditional formal robes and hat to welcome them. It was so interesting and unusual that they stayed for hours.

"My grandmother, Sonam Yuron, made special party food for the occasion, including paba. When the whole audience had been served their food, one of the elders asked whether the paba would be

---

[20] See also the Tale 'The Two Meditating Monks' in this book.
[21] Smanla's mother.
[22] The Dun Dun Chen La is 4800m high and the Lanak La is a little lower. This is a two-day hike for Ladakhis.

33

too big to feed the people singing the traditional folk songs inside the radio, because the singers must be very small to fit in there, but they must also be very hungry after singing so long. Other elders worried if the Balu[23] could be making the music, but they were reassured that the Balu were too big for the radio.

"As I became successful in my metal work I bought a horse for my journeys to other villages and to Leh and to help with the herding responsibilities I still had. My first horse was my favourite. He was red, with a white spot on his forehead, and I named him Spalkar, which means 'white spot on the forehead.'[24] Spalkar ambled beautifully. This particular gait[25] is very important for a smooth ride, and it greatly increases the value of the horse. It meant that when I came home from a party in another village, especially if I'd drunk too much chang,[26] I would almost never fall off. If I did, he would always wait for me. I made his braided bridles and his metal bells, and bought him the most beautiful saddle blankets I could find. The people from the other villages admired my horse and were very interested in the trappings he wore, because they were so different.

"For grazing my herd I usually went to Yerpachan, about an hour's ride from Chilling. Every time we arrived up there, I would dismount and let Spalkar loose to graze. First he always went to scratch his neck on a particular wild rose bush that grew together with a clematis vine at just the right height and angle for the best scratching. One day a snow leopard, which I think had been observing Spalkar regularly doing this, hid there and jumped out from the bushes onto his back. Trying to shake him off, Spalkar galloped away as fast as he could back down to Chilling, and the snow leopard clung on tightly with his claws sunk deeply into his back all the way.

As Spalkar dashed into his pen, the low door crashed into the snow leopard's head and killed him. When we disentangled the snow leopard's body from my horse – he was still holding on despite being

---

[23] See also the Tale 'Balu' in this book.
[24] The great value of this horse is denoted by his having been given a name; Ladakhis seldom name their animals.
[25] Amble: *yurga* in the Ladakhi language.
[26] See also the Tale 'Chang' in this book.

34

dead – we found the snow leopard was missing his tail. We couldn't figure out how that could have happened, until we went back to Yerpachan. There we found the snow leopard's tail wrapped around the clematis bush. It had been torn out when Spalkar bolted the moment the snow leopard jumped on his back. Unfortunately, despite my very best care, my favorite horse died from the wounds made by the snow leopard's claws. For a long time I hated the snow leopard. Once I had bought a new horse I gradually forgot my hatred, but I never again owned such a good horse as Spalkar. We still keep the horse blankets and saddles in Gongma House."

Horse Blankets

Philo: "I would love to see those trappings. A fellow member of the Oriental Rug and Textile Society[27] that I belong to has published a book on her specialist collection of trappings and animal regalia. She would be fascinated to compare them. Also I'd love to see the blanket, to see what weaving and decoration techniques were used. Khenrab, do you remember when we met that trader with his mule caravan and the horse?"

Smanla: "When was this?"

Khenrab: "This happened when the Ladies were walking in the Park. The trader rode a beautiful horse and all the Ladies were feeding and petting the horse except Philo. She was at the back of the horse closely examining the blanket under the saddle. The trader was very surprised. So was I. I hadn't seen visitors being interested in horse blankets before."

[27] http://www.orientalrugandtextilesociety.org.uk.

Philo: "That blanket was beautifully woven with what looked like natural colors and in a geometric pattern. It was a pity so much of it was hidden under the saddle. I asked Khenrab to ask the trader where he'd obtained it and the trader said he had woven it. Intrigued, because I didn't know the men wove here, I inquired, 'Really? You wove it, not your wife?' Snorting derisively, the trader vehemently uttered a brief volley of words which clearly dismayed Khenrab.

"By this time the rest of the Ladies had come to look at the blanket and were listening too and we all insisted that Khenrab translate and promised we wouldn't get upset. The trader had said: 'My wife? Weave? My wife does nothing useful. She is only very good at nagging.'

"Khenrab and the trader were relieved when we all burst out laughing. We laughed so loud we startled all his donkeys into braying like souls in torment. One of the Ladies suggested their uproar would make a great ring-tone for cellphones and YAFCAD should tape this sound and sell it to tourists."

Chang

Khenrab: "Chilling metalsmiths are so highly respected that when they arrive in a village everyone comes out to welcome them with khatas and incense and chang. The chang is always served in a chabskan. The chabskan was first made only in Chilling, then the craft spread to Skiu and Sumda."

Philo: "Does chang take long to brew?"

Khenrab: "Ten days from first boiling – with special prepackaged herbs from the Nubra Valley – to first drinking. The first distillate is blended with a second, third and fourth distillate to reach the right level of taste and strength. It is not possible to drink the first distillate by itself. It is also very good mixed with tsampa. When chang is served to guests, the host puts a small dab of butter on the lip of the chabskan as mark of an especially polite welcome."

Philo became fond of chang mixed with plenty of tsampa into a sort of pudding, which she ate with a spoon. She thought this concoction tasted rather like a fizzy, yeasty poi. Plagued with insomnia, she liked it best as a nightcap, because it worked well as a sleeping aid.

KW 2015

Saintly Shepherdess

Especially distinctive in the Markha Valley are the many long and beautiful mani walls, always to be circumambulated clockwise, on the path heading up to Nimaling. These mani walls are the source of the only story – so far – featuring a Ladakhi woman.

The saintly shepherdess Abi Choskiputit was born in Lungpa House, in Smanla's home village, Markha. Abi Choskiputit's family was very rich and famous for reincarnations of great spiritual masters, such as the head of Stakna Monastery, Lama Tashitamphel, and Chostan Phuntsok, also called Meme Gergan, the teacher of the Sixth Incarnation of Staktsang Rinpoche, the founder of Hemis Monastery.

This teacher and other Hemis monks went for meditation to Anle village, near the Tibetan border, where Meme Gergan died. When a group from Markha village came to collect the body, the people from Anle village refused to relinquish it. The Markha group managed to smuggle it out and returned to their village on foot, carrying the body on a palanquin. The journey took over a month, as Anle is over 300 kms from Markha, with many passes to cross. But all the members of the group fetching the body said that whenever it was their turn to carry it, they felt very light and energetic and had no fatigue at all. The body was kept one year before cremation and during that time it didn't decompose and it smelled only of incense. People who touched the hand of the body for a blessing found it to be moist like a living hand, not dry. The people of Markha built a special stupa to house the great teacher's relics right in front of Markha Gompa.

During her pregnancy, Abi Choskiputit's mother often dreamt vividly, about white glaciers, blue lakes, monks blowing trumpets, and men on horses bringing offerings. These are auspicious signs that usually predict the advent of a Rinpoche. But when Abi Choskiputit was born, the family paid no further attention to her, because it was thought that only a male can be a Rinpoche.

When she was old enough to become a shepherdess, Abi Choskiputit studied the medicinal plants while watching the herd. She remarked that the value of the medicinal herbs harvested from an area in Nimaling that is no bigger than a horse saddle blanket would be enough to buy a horse. She was very intelligent, and although Markha village had no school, she learned the Tibetan script by herself and studied the texts of the Medicine Buddha to become an Amchi.

As she was also an excellent mathematician, the Hemis Monastery manager[28] put her in charge of the accounts for the Monastery's livestock. At that time Hemis Monastery had 10,000 white sheep and goats and 1,000 black sheep and goats, as well as a couple of hundred yaks. Abi Choskiputit was so important that when the Hemis manager came to discuss the accounts, the two of them would sit at the same level.

During her journeys with her herd, Abi Choskiputit began building mani walls in order to maintain a spiritual practice alongside her mundane daily work of shepherding. She brought in the stones by yak and carved the sacred invocations on them herself. Many of her mani walls are in the Markha Valley and in the Kharnah Valley, in the eastern part of the Markha Valley after crossing the Zalung Karpo Pass. Abi Choskiputit spent much time in Kharnah village. A shepherd who arrived in that village, where he had no relatives to help him, wrote a song about her kindness to him there: "She was like my mother."

One summer, having crossed the Zanskar River when it was still frozen from the winter, Abi Choskiputit got stuck in the Alam Valley as the river rose too high with the snow melt for her to cross back over with her flock. She ran out of food and only had wild vegetables and milk from the herd to eat. That year she had the highest number of young born to the herd and the greatest quantity of milk, butter and cheese the herd had ever produced. Out of gratitude she built a stupa in the Alam Valley using buttermilk mixed with the clay. It is called Churku (yoghurt) Stupa, and it still stands in the Alam Valley.

---

[28] The Monastery Manager is called *Chakzod* in the Ladakhi language.

Meanwhile her family thought she was dead and they conducted her funeral ceremony. To feed her soul, according to traditional practice, they burned food (juniper, tsampa and sugar) for 49 days. In the winter, once the Zanskar River had frozen again, she could cross it at last and returned to Markha. To everyone's surprise, she was not only completely healthy and happy, but also had the largest herd they had ever seen. Describing how she had lived in the Alam Valley, she remarked that for several days she couldn't eat at all because she felt no hunger. It turned out this happened at the same time her family was feeding her soul. The smoke from the soul food had nourished her. Now everyone realized that Abi Choskiputit possessed great spiritual power and that her mother's dreams really had referred to her.

After coming home to Markha from the Alam Valley, Abi Choskiputit continued working as a shepherdess and building mani walls – at least fifty are ascribed to her. She placed memorial stones in the walls for relatives, other shepherds, and for all living beings. All the mani walls between Hankar village[29] and Nimaling are

---

[29] Hankar village features a brand-new women's center, constructed by YAFCAD. An ancient ruined castle of mysterious origins overlooks Hankar village. The castle is another favorite snow leopard haunt.

attributed to her. The shepherds of Nimaling composed a song in her honor.

Abi Choskiputit's Song
Singer: Skalzang Lhamo, Marlingpa House, Markha Village

The sun is rising in the east, the warmth and light coming from the east are very kind
The moon is kind too because it also gives light
The beautiful sunlight strikes the glaciers of upper Markha that are like holy temples
The rays of the moon also shine on the lovely glaciers
The temple-glaciers are the source of a thousand springs and streams
As we offer pure water in holy temples, I offer it also to the beautiful temple-glaciers
In front of the holy temple is a garden of a hundred thousand flowers
In front of the beautiful temple-glaciers is a garden of yellow flowers[30]
I offer these flowers to the holy temple and to the temple glaciers for their enjoyment
I offer these flowers every day
From the top of the highest pass, the Kongmaru La, the highest spiritual master is coming
From the top of the highest pass the dragon and his protectors are coming
Please, highest spiritual master, give blessings to this valley of Nimaling
In this beautiful valley of Nimaling we already have plenty of milk
All of us in the valley wish to always have milk like this in the future and forever
The path to the valley is very difficult but the valley is wealthy
We wish this wealth would remain with us forever
In a beautiful tent surrounded by special prayer flags we offer sweet milk
It is in a polished gold pot with dragon handles for His Holiness and the dragons
We offer this to maintain the link between his Holiness and the people of the valley
So he may come again and again to give his blessings.
In Nimaling we have no friends or other relatives
We young shepherds are each other's relatives and friends
Instead of parents we have Abi Choskiputit
The art of Abi Choskiputit's writing on mani stones is pure as gold
Her nephew keeps the barley and so holds a great treasure.

---

[30] These yellow flowers are called *serchen* in the Ladakhi language.

Her reputation for spiritual power continued to increase. Her nephew brought her food while she was herding in the Junglam/Shakam Valley in early autumn. He arrived in late afternoon to find her all alone in camp with no sign of the herd anywhere. He asked, "Where is the herd?" She replied, "Don't worry, they will come," and began preparing their dinner. She never left the camp, and made no summons of any kind that he could see, and yet as evening fell the whole herd came back by themselves. After dinner she said, "Now sleep." He pretended to do so, but peeked out after a while – to see Abi Choskiputit speaking and giving food to presences that were invisible to him. The people began to believe that her spirituality was so high that she could control ghosts, who perhaps had helped her in the Alam Valley and with building the mani walls.

In Ladakh it is thought that if a funeral ceremony is held for you while you are still alive, you will have a long life. Indeed Abi Choskiputit lived to a very old age, but it is unknown when and where she died. She may have died while shepherding in the mountains, in which case no body would have been found, especially as Ladakhis also think that very powerful souls can transmit themselves as a rainbow when they die and leave very little of the physical body behind. No stupas have been erected in her memory as far as is known, nor have any paintings of her been found in any gompa.

Khatas

Coming from Leh by car on the main road, one entrance to Hemis National Park is via the Skurgyal Pass near Rumchung village (four families). Here is a valley filled with stupas and a shrine to protector deities. Khenrab and Smanla got out and went off to perform a special puja. While she waited for them, Philo attached a gold silk khata to her favourite stupa on that slope. She had received this khata on her first visit to Ladakh with the Ladies, and she had brought it back to this valley to bless the work on the Tales. When he and Smanla returned to the car, Khenrab pulled down the sun visor over the driver's seat and took out two white silk khatas that lived behind it in a special bag. He touched both of them to his, Smanla's and Philo's head and carefully returned them to their place.

Smanla: "Happy?"

Khenrab: "Yes, close to enlightenment."

Philo: "Now our journey has begun properly."

Khenrab: "I always keep these two khatas in the car. His Holiness the Dalai Lama blessed one and His Holiness the Drukpa Rinpoche blessed the other."[31]

Smanla: "What did you do with the khata I gave you?"

Khenrab: "Ah yes, I also have a very precious khata especially blessed by Smanla. I keep it safely in this most auspicious location under the driver's seat."

Smanla grabbed one of Khenrab's ears in each hand and twisted them backwards and forwards, grinning at Philo:

"Mechanical Buddha here!"

---

[31] His Holiness the Twelfth Gyalwang Drukpa Rinpoche, Jigme Pema Wangchen (b. 1963), is the head of Hemis Monastery in Hemis National Park. Especially revered by the people of the Park, His Holiness, also affectionately known as 'the Eco-Lama,' is an eloquent and powerful advocate of conservation in the Park.

Two Meditating Monks

Sumdachun (little Sumda; five families) has a temple renowned for its 11th-century frescoes in the Kashmiri style. (The temples of Alchi, Mangyu and Sumdachun were all built around the same time by Lotsawa Rinchen Zangpo,[32] and are all famous for their Kashmiri-style frescoes.) A path over the Stakspi La links the villages of Alchi, Sumdachun and Sumdachenmo (big Sumda; nine families). Sumdachenmo, founded in the 10th century, is one of the oldest villages in the Park.

Two boys from Sumdachun, Rabkar from Pharmapa House and Stanzing Gyatso from Khemtsespa House, became monks together at a very young age. Because Sumdachun's temple had no monastery of its own, each built himself a meditation house. Stanzing Gyatso placed his half an hour's walk away in the upper part of the valley above Sumdachun village in an area called Tsogo.[33] Rabkar established his a couple of hours' walk away, in the parallel Samstan Chosling[34] Valley, between Sumdachun and Sumdachenmo.

When their meditation houses were finished, the two friends began building a line of stupas to link the two valleys. After a while Stanzing Gyatso walked to Tibet to receive further teaching. Meanwhile, Rabkar completed one stupa on his side and continued meditating in Samstan Chosling while he waited for his friend to return from Tibet so they could finish the chain of stupas. Once a snow leopard watched him for a long time through the smoke hole in the roof. It only left after Rabkar blew a ritual trumpet made of human bone to send it away.

---

[32] Also known as 'The Translator'.
[33] *Tsogo*: 'forest at the top' in the Ladakhi language.
[34] Samstan Chosling: Place of Religious Teaching.

When Stanzing Gyatso returned on foot from Tibet after several years, he sought out Rabkar in his meditation house and found him in very poor health. Rabkar had meditated so intensely that he had forgotten to eat. Stanzing Gyatso began feeding him tsampa soup to rebuild his strength, but it wasn't enough to heal him, so Stanzing Gyatso persuaded his friend to return to Sumdachun for treatment. All the way Stanzing Gyatso kept feeding Rabkar tsampa soup, but Rabkar was so weak that it took them two full days to reach the top of the pass from which they could see Sumdachun.

They had both achieved such spiritual power that when they arrived at the top of the pass (which has no name) the sound of a long sacred trumpet reverberated throughout the village heralding their approach. At the same time half rainbows and colourful clouds appeared over the pass. Everyone in Sumdachun saw the rainbows and the bright clouds and heard the trumpet, but its call did not come from the temple. They found its source emanating from a Vajrapani statue[35] in the private temple of Khemtsespa House, Stanzing Gyatso's home. The villagers realized the statue was welcoming the two meditating monks back to Sumdachun and began preparations to receive them with proper honors.

But Rabkar was so exhausted after reaching the top of the pass that during the descent they had to stop after every few steps for him to rest. Even so, at each stop they built a small cairn of stones in gratitude for having achieved the next stage of their arduous journey to their home village. After greeting the villagers, Stanzing Gyatso took Rabkar to his own meditation house above Sumdachun and continued trying to nurse him back to health. However, Rabkar was so frail that he died there seven days later.

A fresco in Sumdachun's temple depicts the two meditating monks. It is on the wall to the right of the shrine room; one monk sits at each of the two bottom corners. Unfortunately, it is not known which is which.

---

[35] Vajrapani statue: Vajrapani is one of three protectors of the Buddha and symbolizes the Buddha's power, in particular that of enlightenment. The name means Thunderbolt (*vajra* in Sanskrit) in the Hand (*pani* in Sanskrit).

Temple trumpets

Tungpo Kyonga

The Vajrapani statue is named Tungpo Kyonga.[36] It still stands in the Khemtsespa House temple, to the right of the main image of Guru Rinpoche.[37] Made of metal and swathed in a red and gold brocaded stole, Tungpo Kyonga is unexpectedly tiny, especially considering its ability to emit such a powerful sound. On its other side is a protector deity, entirely covered by orange and white khatas. As usual, this deity's face is kept covered to protect its power, and it is only unveiled at festivals. Shrines to protector deities are also set up outside villages to safeguard the entire community.

Odzel, the young son of Khangsarpa House, where they were staying, had given Philo a beautifully clear and perfectly hexagonal quartz crystal[38] that morning. She offered the crystal to the keeper of the Vajrapani shrine, who carefully placed it at Tungpo Kyonga's feet. The statue had been stolen once, but the thieves were caught before they could sell it, and Tungpo Kyonga returned unscathed to its home in Sumdachun.

---

[36] *Tungpo kyonga*: 'Trumpet' in the Ladakhi language. Ceremonial trumpets are considered to represent the voices of dragons.
[37] See also the Tale 'War in Chilling' and footnote 16 in this book.
[38] Clear quartz (SiO_2) crystals have great symbolic value in Tibetan Buddhism; they are considered to represent the primordial wisdom of the mind.

Wild Rose Enigma

Both meditation houses still stand. They are surrounded by flowering wild rose bushes which grow all over these valleys. When Rabkar died, the flowers of the wild rose bushes nearest Stanzing Gyatso's meditation house immediately withered out of sorrow. To this day they have never flowered again. Further away other wild rose bushes still bloom regularly, their bright pink glow contrasting vividly with the perennially flowerless branches of the wild rose bushes around his house. The same is said of the wild rose bushes by Rabkar's meditation house.

Khenrab and Philo examined these bushes closely during their visit to the two meditation houses. The ones close to the two houses were not dead, but indeed they did not appear to be flowering. The bushes further away seemed to be fine, and the flower buds were developing normally.[39]

---

[39] These bushes also bear a fruit, whose outer red capsule is consumed in a digestive tea, but the white hairy seed inside is not used.

48

Rabkar's Meditation House

Ishey Chinba, of Kongma House, Archirik village, spent much of his life in Rabkar's meditation house, and attained great spiritual power. There he completed the arduous secluded meditation that lasts three years, three months and three days. He was able to levitate, and he engaged in the advanced practices of inner heat generation[40] and offering his body to wild animals.[41] He died 82 years ago while meditating in the high pastures above Alchi on the other side of the Stakspi La. His body was never returned to Archirik. His reincarnation is the monk Nawang Choldan, from Gatseringpa House, Chilling, to whom his Archirik family gave almost all his religious belongings, except a small ritual drum and the belt of his goncha and a wooden block to stand a hand-turned prayer wheel in. The wooden block, inscribed with the prayer '*om mani padme hum*', is in regular use in Archirik, where it holds the prayer wheel of Ishey Chinba's great-grandson, Rigzen Wangtok. His drum and goncha belt are kept in the family temple.

Snow leopards also visit Rabkar's meditation house, which is on an important snow leopard route; they leave pugmarks and scrapes inside. Scat is found on the paths, but not in the house. The house perches on the edge of a cliff, on the right-hand side of the valley as one heads up it, near a grove of willow trees where a spring trickles out from the rocks, with enormous views over the mountains to the Ganda La, the Markha Valley and Stok Kangri.

Some way below the house is a cairn topped by a splendidly horned blue sheep skull and a large flat square ironstone. It is polite to beat on the ironstone with a rock to alert anyone meditating in the house that visitors are on the way. The metallic ringing sound of the ironstone carries remarkably far. When Philo and Jigmet, Rigzen

---

[40] *Tummo* in the Tibetan language.
[41] *Chod* in the Tibetan language.

Wangtok's son, struck the stone to announce their own approach, a snow leopard sunning itself on the ledge by the house slipped away into the willow grove. This one was shy, but snow leopards seem to be accustomed to human presence around Rabkar's meditation house. Jigmet's grandfather, Meme Paljor,[42] used to take his flocks grazing up the valley and often slept in the meditation house.

Meme Paljor: "Once I was sleeping by the pen and a snow leopard jumped down on me from the roof on its way out – its tail swept my face. I can still remember the feeling of how soft it was – much softer than our domestic cats. Another time, I was sitting there quietly in the evening and I heard my flock begin to get restless. I looked up and a snow leopard was staring down on me from the roof, just like he did with Rabkar. We watched each other without moving for a long time until it slowly withdrew its head and disappeared. Then I went to sit with my nervous flock until they calmed down."

Occasionally monks still use the meditation houses for spiritual practice, especially Rabkar's, perhaps because it is more isolated and in better condition than Stanzing Gyatso's. Rabkar's meditation house has three rooms, of which one is still used as a shrine. The meditation box faces south to catch maximum sun. A small enclosure to protect livestock is attached to the main wall. A round mani structure stands by the entrance. Khenrab and Philo found a spectacular pair of ibex horns by the path to the pass near Rabkar's first stupa, and placed them on the mani circle as they left, with a note to Rabkar and Stanzing Gyatso requesting their blessing for the Tales.

---

[42] See also the Tale 'Arrow Lore' in this book.

Stanzing Gyatso's Meditation House

Stanzing Gyatso's meditation house is also on a major snow leopard trail. It is near a sacred grove of willow trees that have all sprung from the same root, and a sacred spring bubbles up close by. His view is as stupendous as Rabkar's.

Access to his meditation house is impeded by a long but sadly collapsed mani wall. To reach his house, Khenrab and Philo rebuilt part of the wall – without stepping on the mani stones scattered about in the rubble or going round the wall in the inauspicious direction. The cairns of gratitude still line the trail down from the pass to Sumdachun. The valley-linking stupa project was interrupted by Stanzing Gyatso's journey to Tibet and left unfinished after Rabkar died. Four of their stupas are still visible from Stanzing Gyatso's house, although none are intact any more.

Khenrab: "It is my hope that this book will encourage visitors to help restore the four stupas and the collapsed mani wall and complete the line of stupas so that the two meditation houses will at last be linked and finish the noble spiritual project of Rabkar and Stanzing Gyatso."

Stanzing Gyatso's niece,[43] a daughter of his older brother, Ganang Phuntsog, wrote this song about her uncle as she sat on the Spangboche Pass between Chilling and Sumdachenmo. This pass is marked by a dark purple rounded mound between two sharp white peaks, visible from the path to Sumdachun.

---

[43] Unfortunately her name has been lost.

A Song for the Meditating Monk
Singer: Sonam Paldon, Khampa Yokma House, Sumdachenmo

The rays of the sun rising in the east strike the top of the sacred palace
The light of the moon rising in the east strikes the holy Vairocana[44] temple
When I reach the top of Spangboche Pass I see my birthplace Sumdachun far below
Milky water flows from the white cliff above the village
I want to offer it to the holy Vairocana temple
Behind the holy temple glows the protector deity, Sumda Gyalpo, riding a golden horse
In Tsogo I see my paternal uncle's meditation hut shining like a conch shell
In the hut sits my paternal uncle whose cloud of hair gleams like silver
On the right in the big four-pillared room of his parents' house sits Ganang Phuntsog, my wealthy father
In the same room by the stove is my mother, Dzom Dzom Palmo, the steady supplier of rich food, tea, chang, and milk
Among the relatives my maternal uncle, Tunduk Phelay, twinkles like the morning star
Far down my brother, Tunduk Phuntsog, married in Sumdachenmo, glistens like butter
Among our nine brothers and sisters the absence of the pedicularis[45] flower, Stanzing Gyatso,[46] saddens us a little
Otherwise I am very happy to see everyone else.

---

[44] Vairocana (Sanskrit: the Illuminator) – one of the five "self-born" celestial Dhyani Buddhas.

[45] Family Orobanchaceae; the English common name, Lousewort, is rather unattractive given how pretty the flower is.

[46] This is not her uncle the meditating monk, but a favorite brother by the same name, who is dead.

Ladakhi Songs

Smanla: "The niece doesn't mention Rabkar, so he is not part of her family."

Khenrab: "Maybe we should write a verse for Rabkar to add at the end of the niece's song, so he isn't left out."

Smanla: "Old Ladakhi songs focus on the sun and the moon and their gifts to nature. The old songs seek blessings from the sun and the moon to protect nature, and invoke environmental protection for the people. New Ladakhi songs focus on girlfriends and how they look like the sun and the moon. The aspect of caring for nature has disappeared."

False Alarm

These comments arose during a discussion of the monks and a recital of the niece's song over tea and biscuits in the house of Tsering Yangdol, Pharmapa House, from the meditating monk Rabkar's family. She is a widow with two children, a small silent boy and a bright and lively nine-year-old daughter, Dechen Yangdol, who listened intently and punctuated our conversation with eager requests of "Chillo?"[47] for explanations when the spoken English eluded her.

---

[47] *Chillo*: "What did you say?" in the Ladakhi language.

Dechen Yangdol: "Are you sponsoring a child in Ladakh?"
Philo: "No, I am sponsoring a book."
Dechen Yangdol: "Can I be in the book?"
Philo: "Yes, if you tell us a snow leopard story for the book."
Dechen Yangdol stood up and told this Tale.

"A young boy minding the grazing herd all by himself on the mountainside above the village became very lonely. To attract some company, he screamed 'Snow leopard!' This immediately brought many villagers running up the hill yelling and waving sticks to help him chase it away. When they reached him and asked where the snow leopard was, he said it had already fled as they came up. They stayed with him the rest of the day in case it came back, so he was happy.

"The next day he was up there again on his own from early morning and after lunch he got lonely so he did the same thing. The villagers came running, but this time they weren't so happy to be told that the snow leopard had once more disappeared before they arrived. But they all stayed on the mountain with the boy and the herd until evening.

"On the third day the boy sounded his snow leopard alarm again. Just a couple of villagers came, but very slowly and carefully this time so the snow leopard wouldn't see them and flee. Finding no snow leopard, they told the boy they didn't believe there ever had been a snow leopard sneaking up on the herd and he must not disturb them any more.

"On the fourth day a snow leopard did come to prey on the herd. The boy yelled his head off, but both the snow leopard and the villagers ignored him. By himself he could do nothing, so he watched helplessly as the snow leopard stalked, killed and ate a very fine sheep. That evening he returned with the herd and the remains of the sheep and the villagers said he should be ashamed because the loss of the sheep was his fault for giving so many false alarms. He had to live with this shame for the rest of his life. Everybody knew about it and no one ever again gave false alarms about snow leopards."

Philo: "We have a similar story where I come from, but with a wolf instead of a snow leopard, and the wolf eats the boy in the end."

Dechen Yangdol: "It is better the boy does not die, to remind everyone for longer."

Animal Planet

The local youth always clustered round to listen in on story sessions with the elders. In Sumdachenmo village, one particularly faithful shadow, 11-year-old Tsering Dephal, the son of Auntie Sonam Paldon, Khampa Yokma House, appeared in every house every time a Tale was about to begin, silently sidling in and settling discreetly on a cushion against the wall, and quietly slipping out after the Tale was told.

When Auntie Dechen Dolkar, Aktopa House, the mother of Dorje Sumda, the fabulous cook at Camp Husing, finished her Tales, Tsering Dephal sighed deeply, smiled at everyone, stretched, and got up to leave. This time Philo stopped him.

Philo: "Do you know a snow leopard story?"
Tsering Dephal: "No."
Philo: "Have you seen a snow leopard?"
Tsering Dephal: "Yes."

Philo: "When?"

Tsering Dephal: "This summer."

Philo: "Please tell us. It might be good for the book."

Auntie Dolkar handed round more cookies and tea, Tsering Dephal sat back down and Philo reopened her notebook.

Tsering Dephal: "I was walking with my friends near the village and suddenly we saw much movement in the bushes. We went to look and found five foxes fighting about a kill. When they saw us they ran away."

Here Tsering Dephal stopped speaking and gazed calmly at his expectant audience. Everyone waited for him to continue, but he said nothing further. At last Philo broke the baffled silence.

Philo: "And the snow leopard? Where did you see it?"

Tsering Dephal: "On Animal Planet."

Everyone collapsed in giggles, except Tsering Dephal, who looked both pleased and worried.

Philo: "So have you seen a real live snow leopard yet here in Ladakh?"

Tsering Dephal: "No. Not yet. I want to see a real snow leopard very much. But I want to be in the book very much too. If you finish the book before I see a real snow leopard, I won't be in the book."

Philo assured him he would be in the book. This Tale had already flown all around Sumdachenmo village, to general hilarity, by the time they all returned to his house. Everyone still calls him Animal Planet instead of Tsering Dephal.

Sir Robert's First Snow Leopard

"I first started to travel in what is now the Hemis National Park in 1980 and I did manage to see a variety of wildlife, especially birds, but some mammals as well. These included blue sheep, although they were less common and much more shy than today, as well as occasional ibex and Ladakh urial.[48] But, like almost everyone who goes to the Himalayan mountains, what I always hoped to see was a snow leopard. This was not easy. Lack of time and pressure of other work meant that I could not make special trips, so any sighting would be down to luck.

"Also, in those days, the national park did not exist and neither did wildlife tourism. Furthermore, for most villagers, snow leopards were a pest because they were prone to prey on domestic animals. Wolf and snow leopard traps were still found in a few villages, and although these were seldom used, any predator which killed a domestic animal, especially within the village, received short shrift from the aggrieved stock owner. This made all predators, and especially the snow leopard, very wary indeed. For a year or more I saw nothing. Then, in 1981, I had my chance.

"It was late winter. I and a small team of Ladakhi colleagues were travelling through Shang in a blinding snow storm. We were visiting the village center s that the Save The Children Fund ran in the different hamlets up and down the valley and we had also come to discuss various small projects which we had been asked to consider for the coming summer. We took shelter from the vile weather at a house in Shang Nakding and, over warming cups of butter tea, we were told, more or less incidentally to what we would have considered as more important information, that a snow leopard had been seen further up the valley in the direction that we were going. After warming up a bit, we set off again, almost blinded by the whirling snow and frozen by a bitter wind. To be honest, my

---

[48] Ladakh urial: *Ovis orientalis vignei;* a type of sheep.

mind was less on seeing a snow leopard than on keeping warm, inspecting the water channel headwork that we had come to see and then heading back to a hot stove as quickly as possible. I remember, ruefully, that I did not even bother to take my camera!

"We seemed to be the only people out of doors in the empty frozen landscape. But after walking for some time, we met two shivering children beside the path. They looked pretty scared and whispered that a snow leopard had just killed one of their precious sheep and that they were on their way back to Nakding to fetch help in rounding up their scattered flock and, if possible, to recover the remains of the dead sheep. The children hurried off down the path and we began to hope that we might have a view.

"A little further on we saw the snow leopard through the murk. I don't think it saw us straight away. Perhaps the wind and snow and the bad light meant that, for once, we humans were as inaudible and invisible as a wild animal. We were able to approach to within less than a hundred yards of the animal. Even at that range, it was quite difficult to see the snow leopard clearly, so effectively was it camouflaged in the whirling snow and against the brown and grey shale on the hillside. Once focussed, we were able to sit quietly in the snow watching this wonderful animal. Tense and ready to react to any threat, the snow leopard was crouched, feeding, on its kill. It must have seen us eventually but, as we were quiet and still, it evidently saw no reason to leave its meal. The feeding animal seemed to realise that we were not a threat, just other animals met in a snow storm.

"After about twenty minutes, sounds of shouting and the barking of dogs alerted the snow leopard to the news that more aggressive creatures were approaching. Even then it was reluctant to leave its kill. As the noisy crowd came nearer it crouched and snarled, more of a hiss, really. Then, thinking better of resistance, the snow leopard slowly started to move away. I will never forget that lithe shape seemingly shimmering across the scree until the shades of grey of its coat gradually merged with the snow and rock, and the snow leopard vanished into the storm.

"I have been lucky enough to see other snow leopards since that memorable afternoon, but the first sighting of such an animal was very special. Looking back, I think what makes it so is that it was so unplanned, so incidental to our lives. We were not especially looking for a snow leopard. We had no spotter searching the hills for us. The snow leopard was simply a part of the world in which we and it and the villagers lived and there we were together. It was that experience which converted me to conservation, not just of birds and animals, but of a whole way of life, exemplified by the villages of Ladakh, which I believe is important for the world."

Arrow Lore

Archery is a favorite Ladakhi sport. Many village boys carry little home-made bows and arrows. Anything can become fair game for some impromptu target practice. On the path to the 11th-century Sumdachenmo temple, renowned for its free-standing wooden sculptures and restored from a near ruin by YAFCAD, Philo found a lovely long feather. She showed it to Khenrab.

Khenrab: "It is from a dove. We don't find feathers on the paths much; the boys pick them up and use them for their arrows."
Philo: "Shall I give this one to Animal Planet?"
Khenrab: "Sure. If it had been from a golden eagle,[49] I would have donated it to the shrine at the temple. Golden eagle feathers are very rare. They are used for pairs of special arrows. One arrow has eagle owl[50] feathers and its mate arrow has golden eagle feathers.
"In archery competitions, we shoot the eagle owl arrow first and then the golden eagle arrow. This is because the golden eagle chases the eagle owl in the wild. During the day, the golden eagle can see very well, so the eagle owl tends to emerge more at dusk,

---

[49] *Aquila chrysaetos.*
[50] *Bubo bubo.*

when its vision is better than the golden eagle's. When the archery competition goes on into the late afternoon and the light fades, the arrow order is also reversed.

"These competitions usually occur in the spring after ploughing is completed. The two teams in the village are named 'Headman' and 'Monk'. Even if the village has no resident monk, one team is so named out of respect. Pairs of friends are split up between the two teams. If one friend hits the target, the friend on the other team must offer chang and the first friend must drink it – and *vice-versa*. Whoever gets drunker first will have fewer chances of hitting the target and increases the chances of the other side winning.

"The two targets are built of brick and mud with a big wooden circle on which is fixed a smaller white wooden hexagon, without a bull's eye. Any hit on the hexagon is worth five points, and on the circle it is worth one point.

"The two targets are set up opposite each other, and both teams shoot all their arrows at one target, the points are tallied, all the arrows are pulled out and then they shoot from there at the other target. Heavy drumming occurs during the shooting to heighten the suspense. At the end the winning team must perform a victory dance and the losing team must perform a loser's dance."

Further along the path, Khenrab stopped by a young tree.

"Only a certain type of tree[51] makes really good arrows. This is one." He rooted around among the branches.

"The best arrows come from a pair of branches that are straight and growing in parallel from the same parent branch in that tree. It is thought that these arrows make a special bond and reinforce each other in always flying true. Everyone has their own arrows. They are very personal. We will share bows, but not arrows."[52]

---

[51] This type of tree is called *set* in the Ladakhi language.

[52] King Kesar of Ling (the Kham area of eastern Tibet), whose adventures are recounted throughout Ladakh and Tibet, launches a favorite arrow, 'Serda Yuron,' with one feather from the white vulture, one from the eagle and one from the owl. See, e.g., A. H. Francke, *Lower Ladakhi Version of the Kesar Saga* (Asiatic Society of Bengal, Calcutta, 1905).

The best arrowsmith in Ladakh is Meme Sonam Paljor, the grandson of the monk Ishey Chinba, who died when Meme Paljor was born in 1933.[53] Meme Paljor is also a highly skilled maker of sacred ritual drums. So far none of the younger generation, including his own son and grandsons, are interested in learning his craft. In the summer he creates arrows and drums in his workshop in Ezang village (three families), and in the winter he stays up in Archirik with his son Rigzen Wangtok, Rigzen's wife Yangchan, and his grandsons Jigmet[54] and Mipam.

Even at age 82 (in 2015), Meme Paljor still strides around the mountains and collects clear perfect hexagonal quartz crystals along the way. Philo was honored to receive an auspicious trio of these crystals from Meme Paljor when she and Khenrab visited him in Archirik.

---

[53] See also the Tale 'Rabkar's Meditation House' in this book.
[54] See also the Tales 'Rabkar's Meditation House' and 'Teasing Snow Leopards' in this book.

Wisdom Of Ibex

The ibex are a favorite prey of the snow leopard, and their graceful silhouette against the sky from a ridge top adds a delicately elegant note to Ladakh's powerful landscape. So far only Auntie Dolkar (Dorje Sumda's mother) knew a story about them, which is curious, as ibex are considered holy in Ladakh.

"A young, very poor and hungry man asked his rich elder brother for some tsampa for his lunch while he looked for firewood in the mountains. The rich elder brother grudgingly gave him a tiny amount of poor quality tsampa in a bowl, insisting that the bowl be returned to him that same evening.

"Later that day, the poor younger brother pulled up some dry *Artemisia* bushes, and among their roots he found three beautiful ibex statues, one of gold, one of silver, and one of conch shell. He picked each one up to examine it more closely and saw they were carved in exquisite and perfect detail. Sighing in admiration of whoever had crafted them so well, he put them back under the bushes, ate the meager portion of tsampa so ungraciously given to him by his elder brother, and finished collecting firewood.

"When he reached home, the young brother realized that the tattered, threadbare goncha he had been wearing had been replaced by a fine new one, and his slippers had become new boots. In the middle of his hut he found a pile of gold and silver coins. Overjoyed at finding himself suddenly a rich man, he ran out to buy tsampa of the highest quality, filled his elder brother's bowl with it, and returned it to him.

"The elder brother, deeply suspicious of his younger brother's suddenly splendid attire and affluence, emptied the bowl into the cauldron of thukpa, made the bowl's underside sticky with butter, handed it back and asked him as pleasantly as he was able for some more of the excellent tsampa. When the younger brother returned with the refilled bowl, the elder rich brother noticed a few bits of gold and silver stuck to its bottom. Confronting his younger brother with this evidence, together with the premium tsampa, new goncha and boots, the elder brother angrily accused him of theft, threatened to report him to the village headman, and eventually forced the truth out of him.

"The elder brother immediately grabbed a bag, leaped on his horse, and galloped into the mountains to find the precious ibex statues. As he scrabbled among the *Artemisia* roots, all three ibex statues sprang up and scampered away to a high pass where they stood shining in the setting sun and calmly looked down on the elder brother raging in frustration.

"Meanwhile, the younger brother, who was following his elder brother on foot, found himself wearing his old rags and slippers again, and, glancing inside his hut as he passed, he saw that the gold and silver had vanished too. Then his brother thundered back down the mountain and nearly ran him down.

"Despite knowing he was too late to save the ibex statues, the younger brother continued trudging sorrowfully up to the *Artemisia* bushes. As he peered sadly into the empty hole, the shadow of an ibex fell across it, and he looked up to see all three ibex on the pass watching him.

"'Why?' he asked them.

"'We wanted to help you but you couldn't keep a secret,' they replied.

"'My brother forced me to tell, and I tried to stop him, but he was too fast on his horse,' he said.

"'Your brother is greedy and will receive no help from us. But you are pure of heart and we will help you a little bit. So from now on you will always have just enough of what you need – food and clothes – but no riches.'"

Serenity Of Ibex

"I am Tashi Palzum, Gongma House, Chilling. On 22 February 2014 I was accompanying my friend Dolma to Sumdachenmo. On the way we met some tourists and their local guide, loaded with sophisticated spotting scopes and cameras, returning from a trek to look for ibex in that area. They had not seen any that day. So far I had never seen ibex myself, and I was very interested in seeing one too. When we reached Sumdachenmo, I asked the villagers where ibex were likely to be grazing. They advised us to try Samstan Chosling.[55] We arrived there at 9:30 a.m. the next day on our way back to Leh. We had no need to search. Immediately, to our delighted surprise, we saw eight of these lovely animals just opposite us on the bank of the stream. An elder accompanying us explained that they were a group: four sturdy males with large, heavy, beautiful horns and four females with small horns. They had come down early to drink from the stream and were now climbing slowly upwards, searching for food in tiny shrubs, as the ground was covered with snow. We watched them for some 20 minutes. I felt so lucky that day to see the ibex for the first time in my life with my own eyes. I enjoyed their silent movement and I wanted to stay there until they disappeared from sight. But my fellow walkers were in a hurry and kept calling me. With much reluctance I had to leave, turning my eyes back to the ibex again and again, as I could not make my companions wait any longer. From that day onward a sweet memory of ibex made its permanent place within me. The serenity conveyed by their appearance seems to compel me to see them again, again and again … in future."

---

[55] The valley where Rabkar's meditation house is; see also the Tale 'Two Meditating Monks' in this book.

Argali

Khenrab: "One morning in early spring some shepherds from Rumbak village spotted a small group of sheep with spectacular curled horns up on the highest ridge near the Ganda La overlooking their high pasture. They had never seen such sheep before, and they asked a wise old lama if this strange new animal would be good or bad for the village. The lama said that it would be good for the village, and so they were not to hunt the new sheep, but should leave them to establish their herd.

"The villagers followed the lama's advice and soon a thriving flock of these new sheep were regularly seen above Rumbak. The new sheep turned out to be argali,[56] another favorite prey of the snow leopard. Argali are found on the upper slopes of Nimaling in the Markha Valley. This Tale describes their range extension and offers an illustration of the cautious but essentially pro-conservation approach of the Ladakhis, as well as another example of its reinforcement by their spiritual advisers."

---

[56] Argali: *Ovis ammon;* another type of sheep.

Compassion and Conservation

So far only one Tale has emerged about blue sheep. Auntie Paldon, who told it, explained that it was originally a very old song, but although she couldn't remember the tune completely or the words exactly, she did remember the Tale itself, and she thought that it was very important to include it here.

"A blue sheep mother and her two young were grazing on the high slopes in the early evening when suddenly the elder of the lambs noticed someone carrying something long and accompanied by an animal, coming up the hill. The mother saw it was a hunter with a gun and a dog, but so as not to frighten her young she told them that it was a shepherd. The hunter loaded his gun and shot the mother, who tried to conceal that she had been wounded and began nudging her offspring further up the hill, hoping to escape the hunter when night fell. But the elder lamb became suspicious and asked what the loud noise was. His mother replied that it was only thunder. Then he saw blood oozing from her wound and asked what was coming out through her wool. His mother replied that it was only holy water.

"Night fell before the hunter could reach them, but the mother, knowing that the trail of her blood would eventually lead him to her at daybreak, tried to devise a scheme to keep her young safe but unaware of her impending doom. Her pain increased so much during the night that she could not move further or even stand up to look out any more. The elder lamb could no longer be fooled, so she asked him to look after his younger sibling and keep watch and tell her quietly if he saw the hunter coming with the dog, or if he saw scavengers in the sky. `

"At dawn the elder lamb saw the hunter, sharpening a long knife as he walked, following his dog who showed him the way along the trail of blood, while scavengers wheeled in the sky above. The elder one did not want to frighten his mother, so he said nothing. But the young one, unaware of the subterfuge, told his mother and his brother of the approaching hunter, his long knife, and his fierce dog, and the circling scavengers overhead.

"Then the mother urged her young to run away, up or down or right or left, and not to wait for her, because she was too weak to go up the slope and her legs hurt too much to go down the slope and her horns were too big for her to go left or right along the slope. The elder lamb understood, and reluctantly and sadly obeyed his mother, speeding away with his brother. The mother was just able to see that they had both escaped to safety high up on a cliff before the hunter found her and shot her dead."

Philo: "What do you suppose the underlying reason was for telling this very sad Tale? It doesn't seem to have a clear-cut moral, which the 'Wisdom Of Ibex' and the 'False Alarm' Tales, for example, both do."

Khenrab: "I have also been wondering what the reason could be, and I have a theory. I think it is to teach the people to show compassion for all animals because they also experience pain and suffering. In this way a conservation ethic based on shared feeling was developed long before any laws to protect wildlife were put in place. People have to kill animals to eat, but a Tale like this encourages them to keep killing to the strict minimum necessary for survival, and teaches that killing should be avoided if at all possible."

Philo: "So with this Tale it is hoped that compassion will logically lead to conservation by the people."

Khenrab: "Yes, and this compassion in the people for the animals should help make any conservation laws self-enforcing. It is one possible way to deal with 'tragedy of the commons'[57] issues."

---

[57] Garrett Hardin, 'The Tragedy of the Commons,' (1968) 162 *Science* 1243-1248.

Balu

Days at Camp Husing opened with snatches of song emanating from all the Ladakhi tents as their occupants woke up. Philo, delighted by a culture that begins each day singing, listened entranced in her tent until the songs trailed off and the rasp of unzipping tent flaps announced the emergence of her campmates. While everyone gathered for breakfast, one of the older YAFCAD apprentice rangers, Thamchoss Thinless, of Pholongpa House, Kaya village, conducted his daily morning round of all the empty tents, chanting and blowing smoke from a smoldering incense burner into them for general purification and blessing and to expel any bad spirits that might have entered during the night. He then ran round the camp's perimeter, still chanting and waving smoke from the incense burner, to chase any lingering demons out of the compound entirely.

One morning, after a couple of evenings at Camp Husing listening with the other YAFCAD apprentice rangers to Kenrab and Smanla telling Philo the Tales they had collected so far, Thamchoss asked whether they had any Tales about the Balu yet. They didn't, so that evening, over cookies provided by his mother, and after a deep swig of tea, Thamchoss told them a Tale from his grandmother, Samstan Lamo.

"Balu are small male spirits who always wear a hat and carry a stick. Capturing his hat and stick gives you control over a Balu, who has to become your servant. So the Balu take very good care to keep their hats and sticks safely away from Ladakhis, who never kill a Balu but very much like using them to help with their chores.

"Once a man did manage to obtain a hat-and-stick set, although he never explained how. He hung them high up in his house where their tiny Balu owner couldn't reach them, and immediately put the Balu to work. Toiling away under the watchful eye of his new master, the bereft Balu plotted furiously how to retrieve the hat and stick and regain his freedom. His chance came on a sunny day when his master left to plow and sow his fields. The Balu remained alone in the house with the master's grandmother, who was preparing thukpa for lunch and not paying attention to the Balu. After a while the Balu approached her, saying that the master needed a stick to chivvy the dzo pulling the plow, pointing overhead to his own stick. The grandmother left her cauldron, took the stick down, gave it to the Balu, and returned to stirring her thukpa.

"When she was again deeply involved with the lunch, the Balu gripped his stick, peeked around the cauldron, and told her that the master now needed a hat to put the sowing seeds in, pointing up at his own hat. The grandmother gave the Balu his hat. Jamming it on his head, he was instantly freed, and at once he scampered out of the door, triumphantly brandishing his stick and jeering at his former master raging in vain beside his plough in the fields."

Smanla: "The Balu will play tricks but they aren't evil. You want to be careful of the Manmo, though; they are very evil spirits. They will let you die and then **you** become **their** servant forever. When you are watching flocks it is important not to fall asleep, because the Manmo will take you to their village and feed you with stones."

Philo: "How big are the Balu?"

Smanla, putting his elbow on the table with the lower arm and hand facing straight up: "They are this tall, from my elbow to my hand, and this thin."

Philo: "What kind of a hat do the Balu wear? It must be pretty solid to hold seeds."

Smanla: "Oh, the Balu wear long thin hats to make themselves look taller, and the hats have to be made in three angles to fit on their long thin heads. Basically these hats are utterly useless, just as traditional Ladakhi hats are useless."

Ladakhi Hats

Philo: "Why are Ladakhi hats useless?"
Smanla: "I will explain."

Everyone took a swig of tea and leaned forward as Smanla opened his argument.

Smanla: "Have you ever looked really carefully at traditional Ladakhi hats? They are completely ridiculous. They are far too high, and far too small to fit on the head, so they sit right on top of the head, and then they slide around and are always falling off, and they cover nothing except a very small place on top, and they don't protect the head and eyes from the sun and they don't protect the ears from the cold, and they have these useless pointy side horns that stick out and always get in the way."

Smanla emitted this tirade in one long seamless flow, without pausing for breath or tea, and illustrated by lively expressive gestures all around his head. His listeners cried with laughter. Khenrab slumped over his end of the table, slopping tea out of all the cups as he shook with mirth. Philo, giggling uncontrollably, gave up trying to take notes. But Smanla wasn't done yet. He surveyed his gasping audience with satisfaction, looked in vain for a cup with some tea left in it, took a deep breath instead, grinned, and continued.

"And then there is a big problem for women with these traditional hats, because they have to wear them on all important occasions and especially when they serve food and tea, and they can't bend over to serve the food and tea on the low Ladakhi tables because the hat will fall in the food and in the teacups, so they have

71

to hold the hat on their head with one hand and pour tea with the other" – here Smanla stood up straight, grabbed the teapot with one hand, gripped his head with the other, and began pouring tea onto the tablecloth – "all the time standing straight like this and they can't see where they are pouring the tea or putting the food and so there is always a big mess and I do not understand why everyone goes on wearing these traditional hats."

Bodies quivering and whimpering with laughter sprawled over chairs and the few remaining dry bits of the table. Greatly gratified at having rendered everyone in Camp Husing utterly helpless, Smanla resumed his seat, mopped up some tea to make some dry room for his elbows on the table, steepled his fingers magisterially and announced:

Smanla: "Now I will analyze the problems of the perak for you."
Khenrab: "No, please wait. If I laugh any more I will die."
Philo: "Yes, please wait. My sides and head have to quit aching from laughing. And I must finish my notes on your analysis of the Ladakhi hat first. I had to stop writing and then somehow lost my pen with all that laughing."
Smanla: "OK, tomorrow night I will discuss the perak."

Tea house, Martha Valley   KW/NS

72

Balu Lamp

One evening the after-dinner Tale session threatened to be derailed because the kerosene lamp was guttering and Philo needed good light to take notes. Ishey produced the tiniest torch anyone had ever seen, and hung it from a tent support over the middle of the table, ignoring the surrounding doubtful faces. Turning on the surprisingly powerful torch, she said: "Balu lamp."

Wolves And Thukpa

The field training at Husing included recognizing all physical traces of the presence and passage of snow leopards – pug marks, hair, scrapes, scat, urine drops – and assessing their probable age and the likely time and direction of their route. These are essential skills for snow leopard rangers, who use these signs to help them determine where they might be able to observe these highly elusive and beautifully camouflaged cats. Hemis National Park is about 4400 km^2 and, other than the paths between the villages, it is difficult to travel around, especially when tracking snow leopards.

After placing a camera trap overlooking a particularly abundant trail of snow leopard signs all the way up a high valley until it vanished into scree, the group settled down to one of Dorje Sumda's delicious trail lunches. A YAFCAD member, Dorje Sumda comes from a long line of famous Sumda cooks. He volunteered to cook for the Husing field work, and the group feasted like royalty.

Wolves also appreciated Dorje Sumda's cooking. Their culinary interest somewhat complicated camp life for Philo and for Ishey Dolma, a YAFCAD member from Thepa House, Markha village, and the only other woman at Camp Husing. Ishey planned to become the first female Ladakhi snow leopard guide. The two women's tents were pitched away from the other tents at the edge of the compound.

Dorje Sumda's meals were so good that leftovers were rare, but one January night not all the thukpa was eaten, and he poured what was left onto a flat rock on the far side of the frozen river. Later that night, as Philo lay in her tent berating herself for having yet again drunk too much tea during the evening's Tale-time and grimly contemplating a relief mission to the loo tent, something began snuffling, snorting, growling and scratching all around her tent. The sounds would retreat briefly, but were never fully out of earshot, and then they would return close to the tent. The growling was particularly unsettling, as it didn't sound like a fox. Foxes Philo didn't worry about, but wolves and bears she did.

Whatever the creature was, Philo knew she would be fine if she stayed quietly in her tent. She was reluctant to wake up the others after their exhausting day to chase off whatever it was just so she could visit the loo tent. This was not near the camp, but as usual sited well outside the compound down a slope in a small brushwood spinney between the frozen river and the camp. Even after the sounds finally stopped, Philo thought it prudent to stay in her tent until dawn when her campmates were up and about. Their singing sounded especially beautiful to her that morning.

Ishey had heard the sounds too, and had also not considered it wise to leave her tent until daybreak. She thought it had been a wolf. Wolves have been known to attack people and are often rabid; even a nip can be fatal. One of Smanla's grandmothers had died of rabies from a wolf bite. The others in camp had not heard the sounds. On hearing Philo and Ishey's report, Khenrab pulled a remarkable knife from an inside pocket of his jacket. Everyone gathered round to admire it.

Khenrab: "This is a gift from one of the Ladies. It was her father's hunting knife. When she gave it to me I said to her that nothing so good had ever been seen in Ladakh and I promised her that I would never use it to kill any living thing except a wolf, and then only if the wolf attacked me first. I have kept my promise so far, but today maybe I should have this knife ready."

A pre-breakfast educational tracking session, led by Khenrab and Smanla, revealed that two wolves, one large and one small, had eaten the thukpa left out on the rock. The wolves had then crossed the frozen river, "looking for more of Dorje Sumda's tasty thukpa," joked Smanla. They had thoroughly investigated the area around the loo tent, but had not ventured further into the camp than where the women's tents were. Later the camera trap data downloaded from the previous night showed one of them. He was very big indeed.

In the early evening more news of the wolves came with Sonam Gyalson. En route from Leh to his village, Skiu, via Rumbak village, he led three heavily laden donkeys and rode a splendid horse that was wearing an even more beautiful horse blanket than the one Philo had admired with the Ladies. He reported that the wolves had reached the Indus River and killed a horse there.

Philo: "At least they won't be hungry for a while."
Khenrab: "Wolves are always hungry."

Philo cut down on the evening tea with the Tales. Night-time sorties to the loo tent stopped. Dorje Sumda's leftovers were kept for disposal during the day's field work at a site far from camp.

Hungry Travellers

That evening Smanla told a Tale about another pair of hungry travellers.

"After a long day of walking, a pair of travellers found themselves in a village, very hungry, but without money. As they wondered how to get some food, they saw that a funeral ceremony for one of the most revered mothers of the village had just begun. One traveller said to the other: 'If we go and present our condolences in the right way, we might be offered some food. Come with me.' They joined the mourners and soon found the sons and daughters of the mother. The first traveller said to them: 'Please don't be so sad. Your mother is the same as my mother.' The sons and daughters welcomed both travellers and fed them generously, and the two finished their journey.

"Some time later the second traveller, journeying alone without food or money, again found himself near a village at the end of a long, tiring day. He encountered a funeral procession for the wife of the most important man in the village. Remembering how his friend had obtained food before, he went to offer his condolences to the bereaved husband. Approaching the grieving widower, he said in his most sympathetic voice, 'Your wife is my wife.' The widower became very angry and everyone chased the traveller out of the village, threatening to beat him if he stayed."

Dzos And Donkeys

Dorje Sumda: "Speaking of travellers, Sonam Gyalson asked after Sir Robert today."

Khenrab to Philo: "Sonam Gyalson of Gastakpa House is the father of Dorje Skiu, the YAFCAD secretary. Sir Robert always gets Sonam to organize a horse for him to ride and a donkey to carry his stuff for him when he visits Ladakh. Once Sir Robert brought a lot of equipment for projects in the villages. He asked Sonam for his horse as usual, but this time he also requested three donkeys to carry the equipment. Sonam showed up with the horse and one dzo, rather than three donkeys. Sir Robert was still learning Ladakhi back then and Sonam was learning English. He reassured Sir Robert, who was pointing at the huge load and wondering about his three donkeys, like this:

Sonam: "One dzo, yes. Three donkeys' load."

This concise remark is now regularly quoted whenever a novel solution to a problem is proposed.

Amchi Joldan

Amchi Joldan was born in 1955 to a farmer's family of Yokmapa House in Umlung village (two families), Markha Valley, in Hemis National Park. In 1970 he became the first graduate in Amchi − Tibetan Buddhist − medicine from this area. He studied philosophy and medicine in Spituk Gompa under the guidance of Professor Kempo Rinpoche from the Central Institute of Buddhist

Studies, and completed his training in Dharamsala,[58] where he was a student of Ishe Toldan, the physician of His Holiness the 14th Dalai Lama. He became the assistant of the three most famous Amchis in Ladakh at that time, who were based in Stok, Taru and Niey, respectively.

After graduating, Amchi Joldan visited Ishe Toldan every year during the winter to improve his knowledge and practice of Amchi medicine. Kempo Rinpoche sponsored him for these further studies because he considered Amchi Joldan to be an excellent student. After each study trip, Amchi Joldan returned to the Markha Valley with raw material collected from as far away as the Kardung La to prepare his own medicines. He would visit the villagers when they called upon him, and always on his way to and from Dharamsala and/or Leh. Amchi Joldan's medical activities eventually extended from the Markha Valley villages to the other villages in what is now Hemis National Park. Amchi Joldan's reputation in Ladakh was excellent (he was known as "the Amchi with efficient treatments"). He had memorized three of the four medicine Tantras, which was quite unusual in Ladakh at that time. As most of his patients could only pay him with cheese, Amchi Joldan had to farm his own land and sell barley for a living.

In 1975, while Sir Robert was visiting the Markha Valley with a Government Officer from the District Commissioner's Office, the Officer fell seriously ill and lost consciousness. Everybody thought he would die. As he was too weak to be transported, he had to remain in Markha while his entourage went to Leh to find a doctor. Meanwhile, Amchi Joldan took care of him and the Officer recovered fully. The villagers believe it is since then that the Indian Government formally recognized Amchi Medicine in Ladakh, thus enabling 40 Amchis to become Government employees in the area.

In 1981, Amchi Joldan's son, Konchok Tsering, aged 16 months, became very ill. As well as giving his child medicine, he had to do moxibustion. The child recovered, but shortly thereafter Amchi Joldan himself fell very ill. His family assumed he would treat himself, but nobody really knows whether he did or not. In any

---

[58] In 1961 His Holiness the 14th Dalai Lama founded the Men-Tsee-Khang (Tibetan Medical and Astrological Institute (TMAI) or (http://www.men-tsee-khang.org) in Dharamsala.

case, no other Amchi attended to him. At last, when his close relatives realized how severe his illness was, they sent for Professor Kenpo Rinpoche to help.

On his way to Umlung, Professor Rinpochela noticed a dead fish on the bank of the river and then found a dead horse in Nimaling. These were considered to be inauspicious signs, and they were unfortunately confirmed, because when he reached Umlung, Amchi Joldan was dead. He was cremated in a little field below his house, where the rose tree, which usually flowers in the spring, is said to have been covered with flowers, although it was autumn.

When Konchok Tsering, Amchi Joldan's son, was nine years old, Professor Kempo Rinpoche took the boy with him to give him a good education, thereby fulfilling Amchi Joldan's dearest wish concerning his son, which he had often expressed to his mentor. Konchok Tsering became both a monk and an Amchi, educated in philosophy and traditional Tibetan medicine as his father was. Since July 2010, thanks to the generous sponsorship by the Live To Love Foundation, established by His Holiness the Twelfth Gyalwang Drukpa,[59] Amchi Konchok Tsering has been able to visit the villages of Hemis National Park every month, all year round, giving free medical care, and thus carrying on the service begun by his father Amchi Joldan.

Philo: "Have you ever seen a snow leopard on your rounds of the villages?"

Amchi Konchok: "No, I have never seen a snow leopard at all, and I am happy about this. I am terrified of snow leopards, wolves, and bears, and I always carry a big stick to protect myself when I am walking alone."

Philo: "Being scared of wolves and bears is sensible, but why be afraid of snow leopards too? They have never been known to attack human beings."

Amchi Konchok: "I know, but I can't help it. I suspect that this fear is probably a leftover issue from a previous life."

Philo: "Do you ever worry about yetis out there?"

Amchi Konchok: "No."

Khenrab: "There are no yetis in Ladakh, only in Nepal."

---

[59] See http://www.livetolove.org/ and footnote 31 in this book.

79

Temple, Skiu KW 2012

Amchi And Bear

Khenrab recounted a Tale his grandfather, Rinchen Sonam,[60] had told him and Smanla when they were small, one winter's evening, which is when Ladakhi elders tell their Tales.

"The Amchi, doing his medical rounds on the far western boundary of the National Park, was still a long way from the next village when night fell, so he camped in one of the many brushwood pens that line the paths of Ladakh. These pens protect livestock from predators, such as wolves, snow leopards, and bears. The Amchi didn't worry about snow leopards, because none had ever been known to attack a human. He thought this was very noble of the snow leopard, considering how many snow leopards humans have killed. But he did worry about wolves and bears roaming in the region. To repel them and to stay warm, he made a fire with the dry cow dung in the pen.

---

[60] See also the Tale 'Master of Metal' in this book.

"The fire had barely got going and he had just sat down to restoke it when a huge brown bear lumbered into the pen. Paralyzed with terror, the Amchi waited for his life to end. To his surprise, the bear sat down opposite him, slowly raised one of his front paws, palm facing the Amchi, and gestured at the Amchi's medicine box with the other paw. Even by the small flickering fire the Amchi could see the deeply and surely painful cracked pad on the bear's uplifted paw. Moving slowly and deliberately, so as not to startle the bear, he melted some butter in a bowl over the fire, stirred some medicine from his box into it, wound some wool around a small stick and dipped it in this mixture, and held it up so the bear could see it clearly. Then he leaned cautiously forward, thoroughly daubed the bear's cracked pad with this salve, and sat back. The bear contemplated his paw for a while, then heaved himself up on his back legs and shuffled out of the pen, cradling his ailing paw in the healthy one.

"Very relieved, the Amchi made tea and ate tsampa and lay down to sleep. Towards midnight he woke up, intending to feed the fire, just as a bear entered the pen again. The Amchi, at first again transfixed with fear, then recognized 'his' bear. He remained motionless, pretending to be asleep, but with his eyes just open enough to see what was happening. The bear carefully placed a beautiful perak on the Amchi's medicine box, and left the pen.

"The Amchi was overjoyed with his splendid present from the bear and slept undisturbed the rest of the night. In the morning he reached the next village, where he found everyone very upset about a perak that had been stolen during the night. The bear's 'gift' was the stolen perak. Nobody believed the Amchi's story about the bear, and they blamed him for the theft."

Tsering

Amchi And Bear is also a favourite Tale of Smanla's, whose first name means Medicine. He comes from a long line of Amchis. His grandfather, father and younger brother are all Amchis. Smanla's second name, Tsering, appropriately means 'long life.' Ladakhis say "Tsering!" when anyone sneezes. They also say "Tsering!" when someone absent is mentioned, and who then unexpectedly turns up in person or calls on the telephone.

Dakzun

Among the deep and topographically complex valleys plunging down to the Zanskar River along the narrow road to Chilling are overhanging rock faces streaked with a brown-black, viscous exudate that appears to be seeping directly out of the rock itself. This resinous substance is called dakzun. It has medicinal properties: Amchi Konchok explained that it is especially good for headaches, arthritis and pain alleviation. It is usually mixed with other therapeutic ingredients, although for certain conditions it can be dissolved in boiling water and drunk. Amchi Konchok does not think it has been fully analyzed to determine its composition. Philo later found a description of it as being a type of bitumen (shilājeet in Hindi).[61] It seems some animals value it too; pikas[62] and lizards have been observed licking it from the rocks. However, it is extremely hard to get off those inaccessible rocks and it is very expensive. Usually the local people try, using slingshots, to knock off chunks of rock covered with this substance.

---

[61] In: Sanyukta Koshal, '*Ploughshares of Gods: Ladakh*,' Om Publications, New Delhi, 2001, pp. 174 and 406; she spells it *tag-zyun*.
[62] Pika: *Ochotona ladacensi;* related to the hare, with round ears and no tail.

Perak

Smanla: "That Amchi And Bear Tale reminds me – I promised to present my analysis of the problems of the perak."

Under the bright light of Ishey's Balu lamp, Philo brandished her pen and opened her notebook, everyone eagerly filled their teacups, and settled themselves comfortably to listen to the next instalment of Smanla's Disquisition on Traditional Ladakhi Headgear.

Smanla: "First, the perak is extremely costly because it has to have as much red coral and turquoise as can fit on its full length all the way down the woman's back. Red coral and turquoise are expensive, so there is much nagging by the wife for the husband to buy her these precious stones for her perak. Red coral is especially expensive here in Ladakh; it costs more than gold. Coral is easy to fake and it is difficult to be sure when it is real. The husband must always buy the turquoise and coral for the wife. The wife has her own money but she never buys them herself. The nagging doesn't stop because other wives always have more coral and turquoise on their peraks than she does. So the perak causes unhappy home life."

Smanla paused for some tea. He and Khenrab, the only other husband in the mess tent, nodded gloomily at each other. The dismayed young bachelor apprentice rangers contemplated their glum mentors and fiddled uncomfortably with their teacups. Ishey sat quietly, motionless and inscrutable.

Smanla: "The perak presents many other problems. It is huge and it weighs a ton because of all those coral and turquoise stones set in silver on this long piece of heavy leather on the top of the head, crushing the neck and hurting the back. The women can only walk very slowly when they wear it and they must bend."

Hunching forward across his end of the table, clearly burdened by the weight of his virtual perak, Smanla suddenly placed an open hand behind each ear and, grinning maniacally at his audience, who giggled nervously, he flapped his hands and ears wildly while he continued.

Smanla: "The next problem is that women have to wear the perak with these big black woollen batwings sticking out on each side of their heads by their ears, and they can only see forward because the batwings completely block their side vision. What is the purpose of that? I think it is so they cannot look at other men, but that is only my opinion. Also the batwings are dangerous for walking. Already there is the heavy perak and the woman is bending and cannot walk fast and then she can't see out the sides. Then, these batwings are permanently woven into the woman's hair so she has to sleep in them, which is very uncomfortable and inconvenient, so there is more unhappy home life. This is why I don't understand the perak and why our Ladakhi women put up with it at all."

Smanla quit flapping his hands and ears, sat up straight, and drank more tea. Everyone looked expectantly at Ishey, as the sole representative of Ladakhi womanhood in Camp Husing, for enlightenment. She just smiled enigmatically.

Smanla: "See? That is what every Ladakhi woman does when I ask them this. You boys should study very hard to become the best snow leopard spotters in Ladakh in order to earn the extra money because you will need it all to buy turquoise and coral for your wife."

Khenrab: "I tease the women in my family by telling them that every morning when Philo is in Hawai'i she swims in the ocean over this coral. They are very envious."

Smanla: "This is very useful information. I will tell it to the women in my family too."

Philo: "I am not sure how that will help improve all that unhappy home life. But you should also know that this red coral[63] is highly endangered and will only become more precious – and more expensive – the more it is used for decoration. Soon there will be no more left in the ocean. The coral already in the peraks should be carefully preserved, but it really would be better if something that is just as nice a color but not so endangered were used instead. It would certainly also be cheaper for all you men having to buy it."

Family Reunion

Khenrab and Smanla are on year-round, 24-hour call to help when snow leopards need rescuing. Snow leopards can get stuck in places from which they cannot extricate themselves without harming themselves, other Ladakhis, or livestock. So far, Khenrab and Smanla's most satisfying rescue was of a nine-month-old snow leopard that had somehow got itself into the animal pen under the house of the Tarmiktsapa family in Basgo village. Khenrab takes up the Tale.

---

[63] Red coral: *Corallium rubrum* and related species.

"Because baby snow leopards don't usually get stuck in villages, and it was far too young to kill its own food, we theorized that it had become separated from its mother, who should still be in the area. It might therefore be possible to reunite the lost cub with her, especially if we could do it that same day. But we didn't have much time, and we had to drive very slowly with the cub in the car.

"Following our standard procedure for rescued snow leopards, the vet in Leh first checked the cub. Three vets in Leh share a 24-hour permanent duty to deal with rescued snow leopards, so this was done quickly. Finding it to be in good health, he authorized us to release it. Smanla and I drove to a ridge above Basgo village, let the cub out, and watched it stumble through the snow to the very top of the ridge, where it sat down. By this time it was dark. Only just enough moonlight shone to show us the cub's silhouette against the sky. We watched it sit there for over an hour in the freezing cold night, and it still hadn't moved when we had to return to Leh.

"I was very worried and had unhappy snow leopard dreams all night. As it had not snowed in the night, the next morning we returned to the ridge to see if we could ascertain the cub's fate. We easily found where the cub had been sitting and followed its trail of little pug marks in the snow for two hours until the trail finished at a freshly chewed donkey carcass. Higher up the ridge a double set of snow leopard tracks, one of small pugs and one of big pugs, approached the carcass.

"But a triple set of tracks headed away from the carcass, two sets of small pugs and one of big pugs. Not only had it found its mother, but the cub was one of twins. We followed the triple trail until it disappeared. Having feared we would either find the cub's body or no evidence that it had found its mother, let alone that the cub was a twin, we were delighted with the excellent outcome of our intervention. It was the first time that such a young cub had been rescued, released and successfully reunited with its mother."

Snow Leopard Paternity

"Where was the cubs' father?" asked one of the apprentice rangers.

"Cubs generally don't seem to get any care from their father," remarked another.

Khenrab: "That's right. The mother does everything for her cubs."

"Do snow leopards even *have* fathers?" wondered a third.

Smanla: "No, they don't. It happens through high spirituality."

Caring For Rescued Snow Leopards

Philo: "Why did you have to drive especially slowly with the cub in the car?"

Khenrab: "Because we think snow leopards may be prone to motion sickness."

Philo: "How did you find that out?"

Khenrab: "Some time back we had to return a snow leopard to its territory after it had stayed a couple of weeks in our rescue headquarters being treated for an injury. We had a long way to go, the road was very curvy and the driver went very fast because he wanted to get back to Leh before dark. We ourselves were being thrown around in the cab of the truck on the bends.

"When we got to the release place and stopped the truck, the snow leopard stayed lying down, and even when we opened the cage he wouldn't get up. He just lay there, in an open cage. It looked as if he was dozing, because sometimes he would open one eye just a little and then close it again, but otherwise he didn't move. He ignored all our efforts to lure him out. He stayed in that open cage for **three whole hours**. Finally he got up very, very slowly and carefully crawled out of the cage onto the ground. But instead of streaking off immediately for the nearest high rocks, he staggered around near our truck for at least another half hour, keeping himself very close to the ground. At last he gingerly padded off into the rocks, but he still wasn't walking straight or normally.

"We decided he had become carsick from the driver's crazy driving on the winding road and we teased the driver, who was complaining that the release was taking too long. We can't leave until the released snow leopard has gone out of sight from the release place. So now we are careful to drive slowly and not swerve the vehicle abruptly when we have a snow leopard to release."

Philo: "How do you feed a snow leopard when it is being treated in Leh?"

Khenrab: "We have contract butchers who supply two kilos of fresh meat each day for the snow leopard. That is enough. Otherwise it gets fat in the cage without exercise."

Philo: "What happens if you find a dead snow leopard?"

Khenrab: "All the protected animals we find, whether they die in the field or of their injuries when we are trying to help them, are buried on land that belongs to the Wildlife Department. Even if it is a blue sheep and the meat is still okay it is buried. With snow leopards the fur is also burnt. All of this is to make sure none of the parts of any of the protected animals get into the trade. We have a big animal cemetery out there now behind the office."

Smanla: "We've heard that one snow leopard carcass had its canines removed for scientific analysis."

Philo: "I expect that burial site for protected animals would be a good source of information for researchers."

Khenrab: "They will wonder why one snow leopard has no canines."

Smanla: "Big scientific discovery of vegetarian snow leopard."

Courtship and Conflict

This snow leopard soap opera was performed over three days in March 2014. Additional scenes may have been played at night, but the human audience, which included Khenrab, who tells this Tale, was only present by day.

Day 1. Enter a female snow leopard with one of the two cubs born to her in 2012. Enter a male snow leopard, who ignores the cub, probably because it is his own offspring, and embarks on an extended courting and mating program with the female, punctuated by loud mating cries from both. The cub wanders rather aimlessly around the busy couple.

Enter a second male snow leopard, probably attracted by the sounds of mating. Seeing that the female is fully occupied, he tries to attract her attention and disengage her from the first male by threatening her cub. The female now resists the attentions of the first male in order to defend her cub. The first male tries, not gently, to prevent this defense by the female, probably because it interferes with his mating schedule.

By nightfall the first male has successfully mated 19 times with the female despite these distractions, the female has managed to keep her cub safe all day by occasionally escaping the grip of the first male to challenge the intruder male and by interposing her body between her cub and the intruder male while mating with the first male, and the intruder male is skulking around the trio at a prudent distance, apparently waiting for a suitable opportunity to launch another assault on the cub.

Day 2. Repeat of day 1, except that the first male mates with the female 12 times over the course of the day.

Day 3. The first male gives up trying to prevent the female from defending her cub. He confronts and fights the intruder male, chasing him off for good, mates with the female two more times and leaves. The female and her cub lie down and fall asleep.

Khenrab notes that usually cubs don't stay with the mother more than a year, but especially when the cub is female, greater bonding with the mother can occur and the two sometimes stay together longer, perhaps until the cub is old enough to mate. It isn't known for sure whether this was a female cub, but it was too young to mate. This is the first time snow leopard mating has been observed and filmed − by the BBC[64] − in the wild.

Riddles

One day at lunch in the field near Camp Husing a Ladakhi riddle session erupted among the apprentice rangers. Here are two.

Q: "What is very long but casts no shadow?"

A: "A trail."

Q: "What cooks and cooks but is never eaten?"

A: "The wooden spoon in the thukpa."

When she was asked for a Western riddle, Philo offered the one posed as a *laissez-passer* by the Sphinx, an enormous cat-like creature with a human head, to all travellers on the road to Thebes:

Q: "What walks on four legs when young, two legs when middle-aged and three when old?"

A: "A human."

One of the apprentices remarked: "That is a riddle an elder would ask."

---

[64] For a preview, see http://www.bbc.com/earth/bespoke/story/hunt-for-the-grey-ghost.

Tale Testing

When Khenrab and Smanla became snow leopard rangers, they decided to investigate whether any of the Tales they had heard about snow leopards from their elders could be validated. Here are three.

One Tale has snow leopards mating with otters which bring them gifts of fish. This Tale derives from observations of snow leopard pugmarks, otter paw trails, and fish remains left in the snow around the waterholes in the frozen rivers, and hearing the snow leopards' mating cries. Snow leopards only mate in the winter. However, no one, including Khenrab and Smanla, has ever seen a snow leopard mating with an otter.

They have concluded that what actually happens is as follows: the otter fishes in the water under the frozen river surface, comes up through the waterhole to eat the fish on the ice, but scampers away if disturbed, leaving the fish by the waterhole. The snow leopard has never been observed to fish itself, and it prefers to eat its own kill, but it has been seen to eat an otter's fish kill if it is fresh enough.

Another Tale has snow leopards not eating meat at all, but living only on the blood of its kill, which it sucks up and on which it gets drunk. This Tale derives from the villagers' observations of snow leopard behavior in livestock pens: first it kills as many of the herd in the pen as it can, but the only injury found on the animals is a single bite to the throat. The villagers usually find the snow leopard slumped on a pile of carcasses in the farthest corner of the pen, lashing out only if they get too close. Otherwise its movements are languid and erratic; the villagers describe the snow leopard in this condition as "lazy" and ascribe its sluggish, confused behavior to its being "drunk", probably because they themselves act similarly after enjoying too much chang. The pens have no water (or chang), so the villagers consider that only blood from their herd can be the snow leopard's source of a potentially inebriating liquid. The villagers also see that their dead animals have not been eaten, but their carcasses have little or no blood left, and they find almost no blood on the floor of the pen.

Khenrab and Smanla consider that the real explanation is more complex. When a snow leopard enters a usually tightly packed livestock pen, the herd becomes highly agitated and runs around desperately trying to escape and to trample or gore the snow leopard, whose response to this − for it − perilous panic in the pen is to stop the terrified herd's chaotic movement by killing as many of them as possible. The snow leopard's preferred killing method is to leap onto its prey, cling to its struggling body with its limbs and claws, bite into its windpipe and then clamp its jaws around its prey's throat until it suffocates. This requires great strength in the snow leopard's jaws, limbs and claws and a huge expenditure of energy to maintain its deadly grip to the end.

In the wild, a snow leopard would only need to kill like this once every couple of days, and, if it is not disturbed, it will recover its energy by relaxing and eating all its kill slowly in peace and quiet. Furthermore, in the wild, a snow leopard on a kill remains alert, active and focused, not "lazy" and "drunk". But in a crowded pen, heaving with hysterical cattle, it must repeat this killing process many times in rapid succession, and the villagers, alerted by the terrified herd's frantic squealing, braying, snorting and stamping, usually arrive before the snow leopard has killed enough animals to create sufficient calm for it to be able to eat even a single mouthful, let alone rest. By then, the snow leopard's energy is so utterly depleted by its sustained exertions that its "lazy" and "drunk" behavior is comparable to that observed in many other thoroughly exhausted mammals, including *H. sapiens*. When rescuing a snow leopard from such a massive pen slaughter, Khenrab and Smanla usually find it is so tired and listless that it can be captured directly in the net without a tranquillizer dart.

As for the absence of blood in the carcasses and on the floor, first, like all felines, once their canines have grown, snow leopards cannot suck liquids; they must lick them up with their tongue. They cannot suck blood from the throat of their prey, and in a pen context it is impossible to lick up so much blood that none remains visible on the floor either. Next, the windpipe attack usually also opens the prey's jugular vein, and most of its blood will have spouted out from there by the time it has suffocated, leaving its carcass quite bloodless. Finally, by the time the villagers have emptied the pen, all the blood will have been soaked up by and trodden into the straw, leaves and manure on the pen's floor, leaving no immediately obvious traces.

A third Tale is that if its kill is removed, snow leopards will follow the carcass as long as possible, even into a village. This Tale is likely to be confirmed upon investigation, given how much energy a snow leopard invests in catching its prey, and how much the villagers too enjoy the meat of blue sheep, which they do not kill, but whose carcass they will cheerfully take home to eat, even if they find a snow leopard feeding on it. Khenrab received direct evidence in support of this Tale in two separate conversations.

Sonam Dorjay of Kangchenpa House, Sumdachun, a renowned singer of Ladakhi folk songs,[65] who is also currently the headman of the Chilling region,[66] recounted how he came across a fresh blue sheep carcass just as the snow leopard who had killed it was preparing to tuck in.[67] Not averse to feasting on some blue sheep steak himself, Dorjay aimed his slingshot at the part of the carcass nearest to the snow leopard. The snow leopard retreated slightly at the sound of the thwack on the blue sheep's hide, but crept back towards its kill while Dorjay was tying up the carcass to take it home. Another small stone slung in its general direction – Dorjay didn't want to hit it, only to discourage it – had the bereft snow leopard withdraw partially behind a bush, but it made no particular effort to conceal itself and glared at Dorjay as he picked up the blue sheep and set off. Glancing over his shoulder, Dorjay saw the snow leopard emerge from its bush and begin trailing him, halting briefly in its dogged pursuit of its kill only when Dorjay thought it was

---

[65] Like Tsewang Rigzen, the teller of the Tale 'Ancestor Tree,' in this book. Sonam Dorjay also confirmed that he knew no songs about snow leopards, and neither did Auntie Dolkar or Auntie Paldon.

[66] The Chilling region includes the three Sumda villages, Archirik village, Ezang village, and Chilling village. The headman is elected for a three-year, unpaid term.

[67] See also the Tale 'Teasing Snow Leopards,' in this book.

coming too close and unleashed another small stone from his slingshot. The snow leopard followed its kill all the way back to Dorjay's house. As Dorjay closed his front door, he glimpsed the snow leopard crouched just outside, glowering at him. That night regular outbreaks of barking by the village dogs led him to surmise that the snow leopard did not quickly abandon hope of retrieving its prey.

Tsewang Rigzen[68] reminded Khenrab that when Khenrab was very young, he used to accompany the much older Rigzen to watch the flocks in the high pastures. One day they too encountered a snow leopard on a blue sheep kill, which Rigzen hauled back home to Chilling while keeping a despoiled, disgruntled but determined snow leopard at bay all the way.

A fourth Tale, not yet validated by Khenrab and Smanla, is that snow leopards can distinguish, even at distance, between male and female humans, and that they exhibit more fear of and avoid the former than the latter. In support of this Tale it is said that they can be chased away from a kill more quickly and easily by a man than by a woman, and they permit a woman to approach them much more closely than they would a man, although in both cases they will eventually slip away.

Trek ponies   Kh

---

[68] The teller of the Tale 'Ancestor Tree,' in this book.

Teasing Snow Leopards

Headman Sonam Dorjay[69] vividly illustrated the complex psychological relationship Ladakhis have with snow leopards during a long conversation over tea at his house in Sumdachun with Khenrab and Philo.

"Whenever I think about snow leopards when I am inside somewhere – here in my house, chatting with you, or in a friend's house, or in Leh, or in a gompa – I consider myself detached and objective about them. I think the word 'blasé' might be an accurate description of my mind. But that detachment disappears the moment I am outside and I see a snow leopard. Every single time I see one, for the first few seconds I feel an electric shock running through my whole body. It is uncontrollable. I can become detached again after a while, but the initial strong tingling reaction always happens. This animal does seem to have a special magnetism and power. I have seen many snow leopards, and my first response is always the same and always as strong. It has never become weaker over time and more experience with snow leopards.

"I don't feel comfortable about an animal causing this type of involuntary reaction in me, and that may be one reason why I like to tease snow leopards when I get the chance. Taking that blue sheep kill from the snow leopard I told you about[70] was partly to tease it, because of the way it kept peeping at me from the bushes and sneaking up behind me all the way home.

---

[69] See the Tale 'Tale Testing', in this book.
[70] *Ibid.*

"But my best tease so far involved three snow leopards. I was walking along the path and I must have been downwind and walking very quietly because suddenly I saw three of them coming towards me but a bit below me, and clearly unaware I was approaching. I stopped, because that electric shock I mentioned earlier hit me really hard. It was much stronger than usual because I had not seen three snow leopards together before. I had no time to ascertain their relationship. Then they saw me, but only fleetingly, because I quickly ducked uphill behind a big rock, thinking I would try to just watch them for a while.

"They didn't run away, but it soon became clear from their behavior that this was because they were confused about where I had gone, so they didn't know where to go to escape me. Here is when I got the idea to try to tease them. I crept round along the slope above the path while they were still looking up the path where they had first seen me and then I jumped down out on the path right behind them, waving my arms and yelling. Their reaction was hilarious! They were totally surprised and completely spooked. First they sprang up high practically out of their skins and then scattered in three different directions, leaving a huge cloud of dust hanging in the air over the path and three sets of deep claw scrapes in the sand of the path, like skid marks of a car. I laughed so hard I got a bad headache, which I probably deserved, because of teasing them."

Jigmet, Meme Sonam Paljor's[71] grandson, described another snow leopard tease.

"I was riding my horse through very deep fresh snow, which probably muffled the sound of our presence, because on rounding a bend, I found myself right behind three snow leopards, almost certainly a mother and her two almost adult cubs, slowly picking their way through the snow, which reached up to their bellies. They tried to get away, but the snow was so deep they couldn't move quickly. So to tease them a little, but also to watch them some more, I followed them as they floundered through the snow trying to find a more solid surface on which they could run away faster.

---

[71] See the Tale 'Arrow Lore,' in this book.

"What was most interesting to me was the way they used their tails. As soon as they spotted me, all three stuck their tails straight up into the air and then, as I followed them, they began sweeping their tails from side to side in a wide arc. They did this until they found some rocks protruding up out of the snow on which they jumped clear of the snow, and disappeared. I had never seen such a display of tail activity by snow leopards before."

Bayoulpa

At one of the evening Tale sessions in Camp Husing, Dorje Sumda remarked that it is useful to be aware of the Bayoulpa,[72] especially when crossing the Lanak La. He described the experience of his grandfather, Nawang Chotak.

"Nawang Chotak, en route from Chilling to Sumdachenmo, stopped off for tea at a shepherd's tent in the Lanak area to fortify himself for the steep and lonely hike over the pass. Singing quietly to himself in the rhythm of his pace, about halfway down the pass he suddenly became aware that he had entered a busy village. He realized that he must somehow have wandered into the Hidden Village of the Bayoulpa. This is where entities live that look just like Ladakhis, but are only visible to the pure of heart. The Bayoulpa invited him into a house, offered him excellent chang and food and waved as he continued on his way. He felt slightly strange until he

---

[72] Describing himself as standing "at the source of the Indus, in view of certain heights," Dr. A. H. Francke (a scholar of Ladakh and Western Tibet affiliated with the Moravian Mission in Leh, 1870-1930) recounts his "Tibetan fellow traveller telling him that 'behind them lies Ba-yul, the country of tall beings. Only highly developed people can find out something about the life in this Ba-yul. But if a simple man approaches the snowy boundaries, he sometimes hears only voices incomprehensible to him.'" in: Nicholas Roerich, *Altai Himalaya*, Frederick Stokes Company, New York, 1929, p. 108. Philo has not yet been able to find the original story in Dr. Francke's own works.

reached the small hut by the Sumda River in the riverbed of the valley. That is the end of the Bayoulpa territory. Although he walked this route often, this only happened to him one more time, while he returned from Chilling in the dark. At the same place on that pass someone brought him 'a source of light,' which he couldn't describe any more precisely, but it shone until he came to the 'border of the normal world' at the hut. Then the light disappeared."

Khenrab: "The legend says that if you meet the Bayoulpa and don't tell anyone about it you will become rich. Nawang Chotak had two chances to become rich but he was so excited about his experiences that he told everyone and so he never became rich. Everyone in Sumdachenmo has heard the Bayoulpa, but they only know of three people who have actually seen them. These are Nawang Chotak, a Nepalese laborer whose name no one can remember, and a monk. He saw a Bayoulpa monastery up there."
Philo: "There are Bayoulpa monks?"
Khenrab: "It would seem so."

Later, while en route to Sumdachenmo village themselves, Khenrab and Philo stood for a long time on the windy slope above the Sumda River on the edge of the normal world, gazing up the path to the Lanak La and down on the empty hut in the riverbed, hoping to see Bayoulpa. It was getting dark as they left. Not even a glimmer of light flickered on the path up to the La.

Philo: "I am probably not pure of heart enough to see any Bayoulpa yet."
Khenrab: "Not many people are."

In the monastery compound, Alchi

Philo's First Snow Leopard

Philo was beginning to worry that she wasn't pure enough of heart to see a snow leopard, either. Khenrab and Smanla had shown her plenty of snow leopard traces, many so recent that they were still soft, fragrant, tufted with hair and not even sprinkled with dust. Everywhere was so much evidence of snow leopards being about that she began to wonder if she just wasn't looking correctly. She began to sympathize with Alice's exasperation about promises of jam in the looking-glass world: snow leopards yesterday, snow leopards tomorrow, but never snow leopards today. Glimpsing one far away through a spotting scope didn't really count either; she wanted to see one up close and personal.

Late one night a snow leopard padded right by her tent in Camp Husing. Philo was awake, considering how to further purify her heart, when it mewed softly just outside, right by her head. By the time she unwound herself from the three sleeping bags (it was a brisk -15° C in the tent), like a hermit crab leaving a particularly complicated shell, and tried, in vain, to quietly unzip the tent and look out, it was nowhere to be seen. In the morning, with her camp mates, she peevishly contemplated its pugmarks, so frustratingly fresh and close. It was a big snow leopard, and it had even circumambulated her tent.

Philo: "Maybe Dorje Sumda could leave out some thukpa right here by my tent? I don't care about wolves. They don't come in the tent."

Khenrab: "Snow leopards are not interested in thukpa."

Smanla: "Not even thukpa as good as Dorje Sumda's."

Khenrab: "Seriously, though, in our observation work we never set out bait. We do not think it is correct to do this. Also it is not good for the snow leopard. We try to observe their natural behaviour in conditions as natural as possible – given that we are there observing."

Smanla: "When we spend observation nights in hides by paths we know snow leopards take, we put some dried leaves on the path. In case we fall asleep, we can hear them coming, by the crackling of the leaves, but that is all we do."

Philo: "I am clearly still not pure of heart enough yet to see a snow leopard. Thamchoss, please help me by doing a really strong purification puja for my tent and for me every morning, with special chanting and extra incense."

Sometime later, Khenrab and Philo were returning from a Tale session in Sumdachenmo, accompanied by Animal Planet, who needed a lift to Leh. They picked up Khenrab's car at the roadhead, removed the two khatas behind the sun visor and touched them to their foreheads, made sure Smanla's khata was still safely stowed under Khenrab's seat, and set off back to Leh. Khenrab switched on his phone as soon as they emerged from the signal-free zone in the valley at Nimmo. It rang immediately. He listened for a while, spoke briefly, rang off, dialled a number, spoke even more briefly, turned onto the main road and sped off in the opposite direction to Leh. Then he turned to Philo.

Khenrab: "It seems you are now sufficiently pure of heart."

Philo: "Are you going to show me a Bayoulpa?"

Khenrab: "Even better than a Bayoulpa. I am going to show you a snow leopard."

The normally impassive Animal Planet emitted a squeak of incredulous joy from the back seat. Philo, no less incredulous and ecstatic, was speechless.

Khenrab: "A possibly injured snow leopard and a blue sheep were seen by the roadside about 30 kms away from here. This is a rescue call and I am closest so I must go. I called my colleagues in Leh to be ready to bring the truck with the cage and net, and tranquillizer from the vet, and helpers. But first we must see what the situation is."

Even lying wholly exposed by the roadside, the snow leopard was strikingly well camouflaged – it blended perfectly with the stones. Chasing a blue sheep, it had fallen and the two had plummeted down the slope. The snow leopard raised its head and watched their approach. They circled it cautiously. Khenrab estimated it to be about eight to nine years old, in good health, and weighing about 35 kgs. The way it was lying made it impossible to tell whether it was male or female, but Khenrab thought "it looked like a female face."

Khenrab: "I think she has hurt her back. She is not moving her hind legs."

He called the colleagues in Leh to bring the truck, and they settled down by the snow leopard to wait. Concerned that she might develop hypothermia, lying virtually motionless on the cold stones in mid-winter, Khenrab brought out a blanket from the car and he and Philo spread it over her. Philo stroked her long soft tail, which was nearly as long as her body, before tucking it under the blanket. She then went to sit by her magnificent head, and lost herself gazing into the snow leopard's eyes, which were of an ice-blue hue she had never seen, not even in the Southern Ocean, where she had thought the icebergs encompassed all the ice-blues the world could offer. Animal Planet squatted silently close by.

It was dark when the team from Leh arrived. Snow leopard rescues in Ladakh are filmed for the records. Philo held the massive camera light. The team decided it was not necessary to tranquillize her. They put the net over her and lifted her into the cage in the back of the truck. She growled but didn't lash out as she was transferred.

Khenrab, Philo and Animal Planet followed the truck (driving slowly, to avoid her having motion-sickness) back to Leh and saw her safely delivered to the vet. She would stay in the special warm room kept in the Wildlife Department compound for rescued snow leopards.

Animal Planet was delivered to his family, many hours later than scheduled. On saying goodbye to Khenrab and Philo, he said:

"Only yesterday I told you a snow leopard story from the television because I had never seen a real one. Only yesterday..." His voice trailed off dreamily, and he wandered slowly into his house in a delighted daze.

Khenrab remarked to Philo: "I have kept my promise to show you a snow leopard. You even stroked her tail and looked into her eyes. This is a very rare experience. Also you are the first non-Ladakhi to help with a snow leopard rescue."

Khenrab had indeed kept his promise, over and beyond Philo's wildest dreams, and she was profoundly grateful.

But being careful what you wish for is sage advice. Philo had not only seen but also actually even stroked her first snow leopard. The encounter occurred far more up close and personal and under more fascinating conditions than she had ever imagined could be possible. But she had never thought that the snow leopard would also be injured. In the end, she reflected, had she been given the choice, she would have chosen to see her first snow leopard not quite so close, but healthy, wild and free. That joy was, she hoped, still to come. Meanwhile, it was her turn to keep her part of the promise: compiling the Tales of the Snow Leopard in English.

Elegy

Just before Philo was due to set off on her third Tales trip, her mother, Lucy, fell gravely ill. An enthusiastic supporter of the objectives of the Tales project, Lucy ordered Philo to go to Ladakh as scheduled. She said: "I am the past. I have had my life. The Tales project will help future lives." Philo obeyed.

She telephoned Lucy from Ladakh whenever a connection was available. Lucy relished the Tale of the rescue, sent her best wishes for the rapid recovery and release of the snow leopard, and announced her own recuperation and imminent return home.

Greatly relieved at Lucy's improving health, Philo finished her planned work in Ladakh. The prognosis for the rescued snow leopard was also good.

Lucy died, wholly unexpectedly, two hours after Philo called to tell her she too was now home from Ladakh. A devoted and inspiring teacher, Lucy delighted in life, and especially young lives. These Tales, which she so looked forward to reading herself, are part of her legacy to life, and particularly to the youth of Ladakh.

The rescued snow leopard's condition worsened. Khenrab sent word that she had died not long after Lucy.

Jullay

A particularly auspicious day in the Ladakhi calendar occurred during the Husing field work. That morning Thamchoss conducted an extended camp purification and then the apprentice rangers spent the morning clambering about like blue sheep on the highest crags overlooking the camp, attaching long lines of new prayer flags from every accessible protuberance. Khenrab and Smanla supervised from the ground. Ishey kept the incense burner going, seated cross-legged in front of her tent. Philo made some sketches, moving around to capture different angles of the camp, while keeping an amused eye on the prayer flag acrobats capering overhead. Mesmerized by one set of especially precarious edgy antics, which set even Khenrab and Smanla clicking their tongues, she stopped strolling and sketching to watch them with full attention. Suddenly she heard Ishey's voice.

Ishey: "You are very beautiful."
Philo looked down. She had stopped in front of Ishey's tent, her shadow falling across Ishey, who was peering upwards through the clouds of incense.
Philo: "Oh, you are very kind, but I am old and wrinkled."
Khenrab: "Ishey is telling you in the polite Ladakhi way that you are standing in her sun and blocking her view."

And now, esteemed listeners, the tellers of these Tales will vanish from your view, leaving the high Hemis sun to shine fully on the splendid snow leopards of Ladakh.

Jullay…

ACKNOWLEDGEMENTS

The following people and organizations all helped make this book possible in many different and invaluable ways – their contributions are greatly appreciated.

Masood Ahmed
Midori Akamine
Tsering Angmo
Dr. Conrad Aveling
Steve Berry
Mark and Carolyn Blackburn
Dr. E.H. Chave
Sonam Chospel, Venture Ladakh
Rigzin Chostan, Royal Cybercafe
    and Royal Fliers, Leh
Dr. Patricia Cooper
Dr. John Craven
Dr. David Cronan
Tsering Dephal
Dechen Dolkar
Ishey Dolma
Sonam Dorjay
Sir Robert ffolkes Bt OBE
Margaret Garland
Tsewang Gonbo
Daphne and Tony Gotlop
Rosalind Gourgey
Joan Griffiths
Dr. Richard Grigg
Evan Hataishi
Tim Heath, the Blake Society
Catherine Hilton
Nick Hodson for Dr. T.C. Hodson
Juliana Horn
IMarEST HQ Staff (May 2015)
Elizabeth Jennings
T. W. Kalon
Dorje Kaya
Stanzing Kaya
Sam Leigh
Claire Letemendia
Skalzang Lhamo
Tsering Lhamo

Dr. Lorenz Magaard
Dr. Jane McClellan
Philomena Hosselet
Skanzing Namgyal
Esha Neogy
Rinchen Paldan
Sonam Paldon
Sonam Paljor
Tashi Palzum
Tsewang Rigzen
Dorje Rumbak
Dr. George Schaller
Dr. Albert Schütz
Dr. Karen Selph
Stanzing Shingo
Dorje Skiu
Bron and Garrett Solyom
Rinchen Sonam
Ninka Stulemeijer
Dorje Sumda
Swarovski Optik
Drs. Ken and Louise Teague
Thamchoss Thinless
Amchi Konchok Tsering
Jigmet Tundup
University of Hawai'i at Mānoa
    Department of Oceanography
    Hamilton Library
Kris Van Nijen
Lucy and Jan Verlaan
Walter Wagner
Phuntsog Wangyal
Kitty Warnock
Dr. John Wiltshire
Diana Wright
Dechen Yangdol
Lotos Yangsto
Dr. Richard Young and Phyllis Grey
    Young

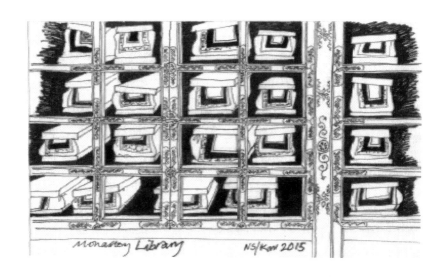

Monastery Library   NS/Kw 2015

GLOSSARY

Amchi: specialist in traditional Tibetan Buddhist medicine
Balu: small trickster sprites
Chabskan: A special metal pot with a distinctive spout and handle for serving chang. First made in Chilling, all Ladakhis have one.
Chang: barley beer
Dorje: metal instrument used in Buddhist rituals; the word means 'thunderbolt' in Tibetan (*vajra* in Sanskrit) and symbolizes the power of enlightenment.
Gompa: Tibetan Buddhist temple and monastery
Goncha: Ladakhi traditional woollen robe, worn by both men and women. It is made in three stages, which usually involves three specialists: one weaves the woollen cloth, another dyes it, and a third tailors it into a robe. Wealthy Ladakhis sometimes wear a colored (often maroon) goncha over a white one, with the white collar and cuffs just visible.
Jullay: traditional Ladakhi greeting that means 'hello', 'goodbye', 'thank you', 'how are you'.
Khata: ceremonial silk scarf that is usually white to symbolize purity and compassion, although gold ones are also acceptable. It is presented on many different important occasions, including births, weddings, funerals, arrivals, departures, visits to temples, shrines,

and to sacred places, such as certain trees, rocks, passes, where the khata is usually left tied to the spot to be honored.

Lama: A teacher of Tibetan Buddhism. In Ladakh, lamas are also monks.

Mani walls: a wall made of stones inscribed with Tibetan Buddhist prayers, especially *om mani padme hum* ('hail to the jewel in the heart of the lotus').

Manmo: evil spirits

Meme: grandfather

Moxibustion: This therapy is from the Chinese medical tradition that uses 'moxa', a soft woolly or spongy substance prepared from mugwort leaves (*Artemisia argyri*). The moxa is shaped into a cone and lit to smolder either directly on the skin or just above it at appropriate points.

Naga: a powerful spirit in the form of a snake

Paba: roasted barley flour which when cooked in water becomes a kind of dumpling, without filling, that is dipped in yoghurt or thukpa

Palu: herb used for house incense

Perak: An extremely heavy and very large headdress, lavishly decorated with coral, turquoise and silver, worn by Ladakhi women. Highly valuable, peraks are cherished heirlooms and worn on special occasions.

Poi: traditional Hawaiian starchy staple food made from the pounded taro (Hawaiian: *kalo*) root.

Puja: sacred ritual or ceremony.

Rinpoche: honorific term applied to a person of great spiritual power; in Tibetan it means 'precious one'.

Stupa: Buddhist religious monument, usually containing sacred relics from a holy person.

Thukpa: traditional Ladakhi dish of vegetables and hand-made noodles, with bits of dried cheese and sometimes meat added; it is usually served as the main course of the afternoon or evening meal.

Tsampa: roasted ground barley flour; a Ladakhi staple.

YAFCAD: **Y**outh **A**ssociation **F**or **C**onservation **A**nd **D**evelopment (of the Hemis National Park).

INDEX OF PLACES

Made in the USA
Charleston, SC
30 November 2016